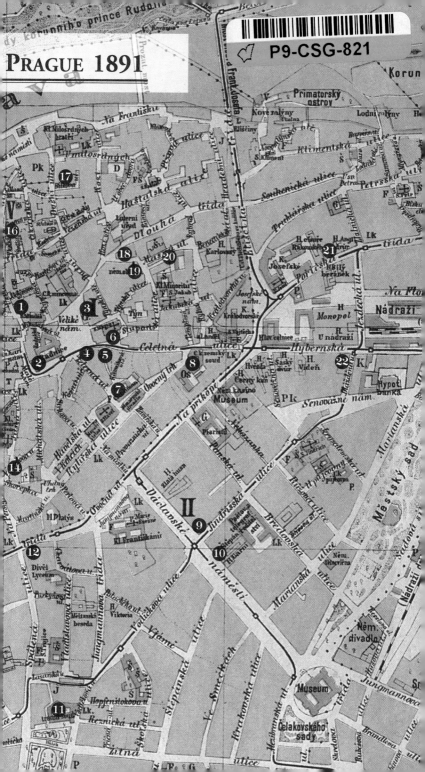

PRAGUE 1891

P9-CSG-821

Vitalis

Franz Kafka and Prague

To get out of Prague. Against the most severe human injury that has ever befallen me, to act with the strongest antidote at my command.

from Franz Kafka's diaries (9. 3. 1914)

Prague does not let go. Neither of us. This mommy has claws. One must get into line or –. We must set it on fire in two places, at Vyšehrad and at the Castle, then we just might be able to get away.

Franz Kafka to Oskar Pollak (1902)

Harald Salfellner

Franz Kafka
and Prague

Third, greatly enlarged
and revised edition

Vitalis

The author wishes to express his heartfelt gratitude to the outstanding Kafka specialist Prof. Hartmut Binder, whose advice and assistance were invaluable.

The photograph opposite the title page (Vitalis Archive) shows the Vyšehrad with the towers of the St. Peter and St. Paul Cathedral.

Editor: Siegfried Mortkowitz
Cover Photo: Ivan Koreček
Typesetting: Cadis, Praha
Print: Finidr, Český Těšín

ISBN 80-85938-35-9

TABLE OF CONTENTS

PREFACE

When Franz Kafka was buried in the presence of a small group of his relatives and friends, the inhabitants of his hometown, Prague – even in circles in which he was not unknown – did not have the slightest notion that one of the great writers of this century had passed away. A commemorative hour at the "Kleine Bühne" [a Prague theatre], attended by friends and colleagues, also did not produce any premonition of his future greatness. His Czech contemporaries learned of his death from a few lines written by Milena Jesenská.

What actually comprises the phenomenon that the work of the Praguer Franz Kafka has become? The living conditions so characteristic of so many gifted individuals from this city and nation? His destiny, shared by so many others from Prague, Brno, Liberec and even the Moravian city of Ostrava, who at first did not receive any recognition of their genius in their native land and had to reap their success beyond the border and were therefore not regarded as Praguers for some time? In Vienna, in Zürich or in Berlin they were classified as Austrians. At that time, what did the Kleist Prize, which Kafka received, signify in the gatherings of the Prague literati? Here, the pedigree of a traditional clan was often decisive. In the cafés – the Concordia, the Arco – with theatre and concert audiences, the work itself always ran the risk of being classified as regional literature.

It would probably have taken too long for Kafka's greatness to be recognized had his friend Max Brod not preserved Kafka's writings and called attention to their literary significance. Equally undisputed is the fact that Kafka's work first received a mixed reception after his death. In the then young nation, all of the German-language writers had their legitimate places in the various circles of their like-minded ideologies. There, the press and public were at their service. If they were like Rilke, Werfel, Kraus and all the others already long in Vienna, Munich or Switzerland – or, like Egon Erwin Kisch, always on the road – then they merely made guest appearances in their native Prague, held literary audience in the Continental or, occasionally after the theatre, in the Café Slávia.

It would still take some time before interest in Franz Kafka first sprang up in Prague. It could have been in the autumn of 1931. During one of his many well-attended readings, the animated German scholar Professor Herbert Cysarz, then from the German University, responded to a question from the audience by gesturing like a literary pundit and declaring, "And Kafka? A Jewish classic."

A second world war had to come over Europe, the insular, education-keen Prague Germans had to vanish from the picture, until Kafka's hometown began to remember him. The principal interpreters in post-war Germany were the new American citizens, emigrants and recent authors who had settled in the Western Hemisphere. They came to Prague and enlightened the indigenous in diverse fashion on Kafka. They visited the grandchildren of Kafka's housekeeper, his cleaning women and the few survivors of the Holocaust. If the experts stemmed from the West, then Kafka's works were apodictically categorized in the literary order as follows: Kafka was a German-language Czech of Jewish descent with a German education. He spoke both of his German mother-tongue and of his heartfelt sympathies for his Czech fellow-citizens. The Czechs themselves, however, remained cool. In Prague, no one was yet claiming him as their own. Many arguments were put forward against it. It was not yet the time to elevate Prague to the level of a literary casualty ward. In addition, information from East Berlin, which alluded to the new political brotherhood on the Vltava, produced a chilly disaffection and even led to a rejection of Kafka. There was a great deal of talk about decadence and alienation. It is certainly part of that era's absurdity that the official theatre of the peoples' regime in

Prague received its orders about which author to recognize from East Berlin ideologues.

Of course, Kafka's work and its charisma could not be repressed – not even in Prague. There followed conferences, for example that in Liblice, where Kafka was discussed by defender and judge. How many hours of discussion by the ruling party's central committee were necessary to determine the number of participants and even the seating arrangements at table! Stormy debates were held over whether foreign German scholars would be allowed to appear. On the other hand, native scholars, who wielded undisputed power in the German language, were forbidden to use it. The number of Czech interpreters of Kafka's work was strictly limited. After the fall of the Iron Curtain, it came out that many of those concerned had been under scrutiny by the secret police.

And Max Brod still lived far from Prague, in Tel Aviv. His participation, as the legitimate administrator of Kafka's legacy, was out of the question at that time. He did not appear until 1964, shortly before the Prague Spring. The former state official of the First Republic held his lecture in Czech, before hundreds of readers and admirers of Kafka's work, in the banquet hall of the Strahov Monastery. He was loudly acclaimed, and there was talk of Franz Kafka's return to his hometown. Later, that day would be described as a harbinger of the 1968 Prague Spring.

So it did not surprise an observer from those years that a young intellectual from Graz, Austria, settled down in Prague, Kafka's hometown – as author and publisher. The former physician Harald Salfellner is Austrian and therefore not subject to the occasional distance to Franz Kafka that so often leaves German literary scholars helpless. Max Brod once said of himself that he and Kafka were actually Prague Austrians. Harald Salfellner has moved into the Czech capital's literary scene and has learned the Czech language – and uses it. His book about Franz Kafka is therefore no new Baedeker, no vade mecum for the new tourism industry. He has gone his own way with Franz Kafka, along the route of Kafka's life in

Prague. Harald Salfellner brings to this task something that many other interpreters surely lack. It is the way to the Czech language, the vernacular of that world in which Franz Kafka lived and which must be understood.

Salfellner's work as publisher in this city consciously continues the literary tradition that has been customary here since the days of Rudolf II and which is not chiefly directed at foreign visitors. The libraries of Czech scholars of all disciplines contain a not inconsiderable number of works in the German language. Today as well.

Herein lies the indigenous symbiosis of this city. It is represented by the masters of the meeting of the two languages – Pavel Eisner, Otakar Fischer, Otto Pick, O. F. Babler. And here also begins Harald Salfellner's book, which of necessity must lead to an understanding of Franz Kafka: It teaches us to see Prague as Franz Kafka saw it.

Hugo Rokyta
Prague, 1998

Franz Kafka's Prague

With 230,000 inhabitants (1910), the Prague of Franz Kafka's time was the third-largest city of the Habsburg Empire. If we include the inhabitants of the suburbs, the population of Prague came to about 600,000. Around 1880, however, Prague had no more than 310,000 inhabitants in all. Thus, the population of Prague had virtually doubled in 30 years.

> According to the last census, the population of Prague consists of 90.7% Czechs and 9.3% Germans, and in the suburbs 93.1% Czechs and 6.9% Germans. Actually, the majority of the inhabitants of Prague, especially those in business circles, speak both Czech and German. In the better hotels and restaurants as well as in the larger shops German is everywhere understood; also coachmen, porters and luggage carriers at the railway station as a rule understand as much German as they need in their contact with foreigners.
>
> *Griebens Reiseführer Prag,* 1911

Culturally and economically speaking, Germans and Jews made up only a small, yet indisputably important, part of the city. About 32,000 Germans lived in Prague at this time.

> They were almost exclusively upper middle-class, owners of the brown-coal pits, administrative officials of the Montan enterprises and the Škoda weapons factory, hops traders who travelled back and forth between Saaz and North America, sugar-, textile- and paper-manufacturers as well as bank directors; their circles were frequented by professors, high officers and government employees. Such a thing as a German proletariat hardly existed.
>
> Egon Erwin Kisch

The former New German Theatre, today the State Opera

The small minority of German-speaking Praguers, many of
them of Jewish descent, counted among their assets two major
theatres, a university, a college of technology, a concert hall, a
half-dozen secondary schools and several daily newspapers of
more than regional importance.

> Prague newspapers published in German: the two dailies
> *Bohemia* and *Prager Tagblatt* (two issues each weekday),
> then the *Deutsches Abendblatt* and the *Montagsblatt aus
> Böhmen*. The government newspaper, the *Prager Abend-
> blatt*, appears weekdays. There is also a Czech newspaper
> in German, *Die Union*. The other (political-party) pa-
> pers will be of no interest to the foreigner.
>
> *Griebens Reiseführer Prag,* 1911

Prague's German-language poets and writers had access to at least four ethnic sources at once: the German, of course, to which they belonged culturally and linguistically; the Czech, which surrounded them everywhere as an element of life; the Jewish – even if they themselves were not Jewish – since it formed an historic, ubiquitously palpable factor of the city; and the Austrian, within which they were all born and raised and which also fatefully influenced them, whether they merely affirmed it or found fault with this or that in it.

Johannes Urzidil, *There Goes Kafka*

A street scene from the Prague Jewish ghetto (around 1898)

At the end of the 19th century, Prague experienced very fundamental changes in its landscape. Around 1888, the community purchased the earthworks between the districts of the Prague New Town and Vinohrady, which merged after the walls were removed and the divided plots of land were sold to private individuals. There were also important changes made to the Old Town during Kafka's lifetime.

15

With the onset of the migration of affluent Jews into other city districts, after Emperor Joseph II had issued his Tolerance Edict, and the immigration of penniless lower-class groups as well as all manner of shady riff-raff, Prague's Jewish ghetto – on the periphery of which stood the house in which Kafka was born – increasingly degenerated into a poor quarter in the heart of the city in which low dives, prostitution and crime proliferated. While, in 1890, the adjacent Old Town contained only 644 people per hectare, and the figure for the growing district of Žižkov was 1,300, in Josefov an average of 1,822 people were packed into each hectare.

An initial bill from the year 1855 called for a "clean-up" of the run-down and desperately overpopulated Prague Jewish quarter. It was hoped that, with the tearing down of the ancient Jewish district and parts of the Old Town outside the Jewish ghetto, the misery and desperate hygienic conditions, a constant nest of various epidemics, would be eradicated. With the basic clean-up, which was carried out in 1890 after countless meetings and resolutions, most of the historic building stock unfortunately also fell victim to the all-too-boldly swung pickaxe. For sanitary reasons, the end now came to the thousand-year-old settlement. In place of the dark and twisting streets of the poor now came the modern Art Nouveau palaces of the prosperous bourgeoisie.

A large majority of Prague's Jewish population supported the clean-up, since the ghetto had become a symbol of centuries of discrimination. The thousand-year-old ghetto was torn down not only for reasons of hygiene, however, but above all because the bourgeoisie, which had become rich in the course of industrialisation, needed space for the building plans of the *Gründerzeit*, a period of rapid industrial expansion in Germany.

During Kafka's lifetime Prague was anything but a sleepy provincial town.

Streets of the Prague Jewish ghetto (around 1898)

Cubist lamppost on Jungmannovo náměstí

In 1898, the first significant *Jugendstil* (Art Nouveau) exhibitions took place in the Topič Salon. Less than a decade later, the group *Osma* (The Eight), the first association of modern artists (whose members included Bohumil Kubišta, Emil Filla, Otokar Kubín, as well as Friedrich Feigl and Willy Nowak, highly appreciated by Kafka) presented themselves to the public.

More than 200 clubs nurtured an active social life in the German House. In 1895, at the initiative of Emil Orlík, among others, the Association of German Artists was founded.

The former „Deutsches Haus" (German House) on the street Na Příkopě; since 1945, „Slovanský dům" (Slavic House)

Its weekly Thursday evening meetings were attended by such writers as Oskar Wiener, Rainer Maria Rilke and Paul Leppin.

But also on the Czech side, creative powers long repressed found expression in important cultural achievements. Czech Prague embraced everything from Munch to French Cubism; in contrast to Vienna, Cubism held full sway in Prague. The Germans, on the other hand, flew the banner of Expressionism.

The transformation of the city and its life advanced dramatically and affected all essential spheres of life.

Trade and industry experienced a tremendous upsurge. Telephones began to replace obsolete communications technology, power stations made the operation of modern technical equipment possible, cable cars and the first automobiles heralded a future revolution in transportation.

> Large industrial enterprises have acquired an international reputation. This was followed by the development of a transportation system of which Prague forms the main railway junction of Bohemia. Further progress is in the offing through the canalisation of the Moldau [Vltava], which will make Prague the starting point for shipping on the Moldau and the Elbe.
>
> *Griebens Reiseführer Prag,* 1911

A wagon from the first electric streetcar on Letná hill, 1891

Electric power station in Prague-Holešovice

The young boy Franz Kafka must have observed with great astonishment an event to which his environment paid fitting attention: In 1894, Prague was illuminated by electricity. Direct current to the lamps was delivered by a small electric facility, the first electricity plant in Bohemia. The municipal electric power station in Žižkov did not begin operating until one

Turbine room

year later, in 1895. That is the reason the first electric tram, which ran between the Letna heights and Královské obory beginning in 1891, had to be powered by the entrepreneur Křižík – who a few years earlier had  moved his factory from Plzeň to Prague-Karlín – with his own provisional power station. Later, in 1903, Křižík also electrified the first Bohemian railway (between Tábor and Bechyně).

In 1899, the central Prague electrical station in Holešovice (ústřední elektrická stanice), which had been equipped by the Electro-Technical Stock Company (formerly Kolben & Co.), the Ringhoffer Company, the Akciová strojírna (formerly Breitfeld und Daněk), among others, began operating.

These and the many other consequences of technical progress could certainly not have remained concealed from Franz Kafka. One can gather from his diaries how very much he was fascinated by aeronautics (which, in the truest sense of the word, opened up new horizons for humanity,) and cinematography. Beginning in 1907, Prague had a full-time cinema, the *Biograph Ponrepo* at Karlová 20. At the time, cinema was little more than relatively simply filmed theatre. However, Kafka – who could summon up little sympathy for music but therefore all the more enthusiasm for moving pictures – loved going to the "picture-theatre". He would then discuss with his friend Max Brod what he had

seen, and occasionally wrote down his observations in his diary.

However, Kafka's Prague was not only a city which was blooming as a result of the blessings of technological progress, but was also a place of bitter social conflict. Mass demonstrations by revolutionary workers, who had begun to demand political power, were a palpable sign of the latent dissatisfaction. In addition to being a city of high style, Prague was also a place of misery and poverty, a consequence of the very developments that would come to characterise the twentieth century so crucially . And in Prague the centuries-old national conflicts between Czechs and Germans were fought with fierce determination:

> The last decades in Prague have been characterised by a constant repression of the German element. After the last German member vanished from the municipal government in the 1880s, the battle against all things German in public life has been crowned with rapid success. Wherever possible, the Czech language was given predominance or monopoly, the new Czech Technical University (1868) was established, and at parties, in the newspapers and parliamentary debates, hatred of Germans was fiercely evoked. All this erupted in 1897 in the form of violence in the streets of Prague, forcing the government to declare a state of emergency. From then on, unrest in the streets has repeatedly made official intervention necessary; the conflict rages on in the parliamentary sessions.
>
> *Griebens Reiseführer Prag,* 1911

Long before the turn of the century, the Czech-German contradiction had already developed into a (not always only) verbal war of position in which the in any case rare words of reason or moderation were drowned out by the shouts of the nationalistic rabble on both sides. The first stages of a Czech national consciousness, at the beginning of the 19th century, were based on the works of Czech scholars who had written in German. Among them was the linguist and literary scholar

Josef Dobrovský, who can be considered the creator of modern Czech. By the end of the century, such a "being above things" had become inconceivable. Political liberalism had apparently had its day: On the Czech side, a party named "Mladočeši" (Young Czechs) had entered the conflict. They did not think twice about running in the parliamentary elections of spring 1897 with

New Czech street-sign over mixed-language inscription (from 1912)

such an unbridled anti-Semite as Václav Březnovský. Attitudes also increasingly hardened on the German side.

Mass meeting of the national gymnastics association „Sokol" on Old Town Square (around 1912)

The reaction to the language law enacted by the former governor of Galicia, Kazimierz Graf Badeni, who in 1895 was entrusted by Emperor Franz Joseph to set up a "government with a strong hand", illustrated that every basis for discussion between the country's two language groups had been lost long before. Badeni, who had to push forward the income tax legislation and lead budget negotiations with Hungary, attempted to achieve the necessary truce via various concessions. Approximately one month after assuming his post, he suspended the state of emergency that had been imposed in Prague two years earlier. He hoped to motivate the persistently obstructionist Young Czechs – who had been represented in the Vienna Parliament since 1891 and had become the most important Czech force – to agree to constructive parliamentary cooperation by implementing a voting-rights reform, which he pushed through the *Reichsrat* in June 1896. But Badeni was forced to admit that only concessions in the area of Czech language demands would bring results. He therefore enacted language laws for Bohemia on April 5, 1897 (followed three weeks later by similar laws for Moravia), which produced violent reactions and even led to a national crisis.

According to the Badeni Decrees, which were enacted without any consultation with representatives of the Bohemian Germans, German and Czech had equal footing in official communications in the Bohemian crownlands. For a German official in a German-language city such as Reichenberg (Liberec), this meant that he was forced to learn the Czech language if he wanted to have a career in the civil service. What this signified to the Geman-speaking population in the area later known as the *Sudetenland* – in which there already were a large number of Czech civil servants – can only be understood if one considers both the people's self-perception and their fears, and if one remembers that they had expected assistance from Vienna in this ethnic conflict and now felt that they had been sold out. However, one must not overlook the fact that the Czechs had had to accept German as the official language for centuries – even in purely Czech-populated areas.

The protests and mass demonstrations, whose intensity exceeded all expectations, shook not only the country's large German cities, such as Reichenberg, Karlsbad (Karlovy Vary) and Teplitz (Teplice), but also German areas in all of "Cisleithanien" up to faraway alpine Graz. In the German areas of Bohemia, acts of violence were committed against the Czech minority. Even in the Vienna Reichstag, in whose parliamentary negotiations the bitter conflict also raged, propriety was thrown to the winds: where discussion failed, a cocked fist was always a political option.

A symbol of old Austria: the Radetzky Memorial on Malostranské náměstí (removed after establishment of the First Republic)

Prague chestnut roaster (around 1890)

In this dangerous situation, Emperor Franz Joseph had no other choice but to close down Parliament (on November 28, 1897) and dismiss Badeni. In December of the same year, the Czechs gave vent to their frustrations in the streets of Prague through furious anti-German and anti-Semitic violence, which the Young Czech politicians – unlike the Social Democrats – watched without taking any action. This anarchic street lunacy did not end until martial law was imposed.

> At the time Kafka produced his major works, Prague was most typically Prague and also most typically kafkaesque. One can understand and define the essence of Prague more fully through Kafka than through any other author – and definitely better through him than any Czech work from that time, although the latter must have made it a fashion to portray Prague. This is perhaps also one of the involuntary reasons that, on the Czech side, attempts are constantly made to depict Kafka as a kind of disguised Czech and to spirit him away from German literature. These attempts are well served by, among others, the American definition of nationality by nation of birth and thereby categorizes Kafka now and again as a "Czech writer". This is, of course, utter nonsense, for a writer belongs to the representation of the

language in which he thinks and writes. If Kafka once wrote to his Czech friend Milena Jesenská, "German is my native language and therefore comes naturally to me, but Czech is far more endearing", it must be taken into account that this sentence should not be evaluated as a "literary statement" but that it was sent to a Czech beloved and written to suit her.

Johannes Urzidil, *There Goes Kafka*

Now I am going to say something silly about the same thing, i.e. what is silly is that I say something that I consider to be right without considering that it hurts me. And then Milena speaks of anxiety, punches me in the chest and asks something that is absolutely the same in Czech in gesture and in tone: *jste žid?* [Are you Jewish?] Don't you see how in *jste* the fist is drawn back to gather strength? And in *žid* the punch flies forward, willingly and unfailingly? Such are the side-effects that the Czech language often has for the German ear.

For example, you once asked how it is that I make my stay here contingent on a letter, and you yourself answered: *nechápu* [Czech for I don't understand]. An exotic word in Czech and even in your pronunciation, it is so severe, apathetic, cold-eyed, spare and, above all,

View of Manés Bridge and the Prague Castle

nutcracker-like, the word makes the jaws crash against each other three times, or more correctly: the first syllable attempts to grasp the nut, then the second syllable wrenches the mouth wide open, now the nut fits, and the third syllable finally cracks, do you hear the teeth?

Franz Kafka to Milena Jesenská (1920)

In this battle of language and nationality, the orientation of the Jewish people in Prague was mixed.

While urban liberal Jews identified themselves essentially as Germans, Jews streaming in from the surrounding areas felt themselves to be Czech. The businessman Hermann Kafka (Franz's father) struck a pragmatic course in this labyrinth of nationalistic sentiments. His determination to rise socially produced the obvious desire to belong to the small German upper class. However, his business was left unaffected during the anti-German riots of the 1890s. The name Kafka provided the family with sufficient Czech atmosphere.

Relief on the coat of arms on the Jewish Town Hall

You could, for instance, rail at the Czechs, then at the Germans, then at the Jews, and not only selectively but in every respect, and finally no one was left but you. For me, you took on that enigmatic something that all tyrants have whose law is founded in their person, not their reasoning.

Franz Kafka,
Letter
to his Father

The central administrative authorities in Vienna were thoroughly aware of this tense situation. Thus, Prague was governed by decree throughout these years. The essentially supranational imperial family was not able to meet the demands of a newly dawning age. A change, as yet unclearly defined, lay ahead. The multi-ethnic monarchical state had had its day; it was regarded as a prison of nations. But for the time being the future hid what it had in store.

Franz Kafka was born in the capital of the Kingdom of Bohemia. The term *kingdom* represented the world of the old Austria and became a symbol for something passing, antiquated, lifeless. For many German inhabitants Prague was therefore also a "dead city" of dreams and myth. The Czechs felt differently, since the future lay open to them.

However, the city, both lovingly and derisively also referred to as the "Schmockkästchen of the monarchy", was an Austrian microcosm as well. By the time Franz Kafka died, this old Austria was already a thing of the past. The modern period, long anticipated, had begun October 28, in 1918, with the creation of the First Republic. The Praguer Franz Kafka, born a subject of his imperial-royal apostolic Majesty, died a citizen of the Czechoslovak Republic of T. G. Masaryk. The old Prague seemed to have been transformed overnight into a completely new city which, on the surface, rapidly changed under the influence of fashion, trends and developments. These serious changes, however, could not destroy the essence of the city.

And even if every generation dreams of a Prague that is supposed to have existed and will never exist again, it may nevertheless be asserted that this city, Kafka's Prague, in its inner being, has remained untouched and timeless to this day and above and beyond all ruptures. And precisely this characteristic feature is also relevant for Franz Kafka's lifework. Perhaps this provides an additional reason to meet this writer right in his hometown, for Franz Kafka and his Prague are timeless.

1883 – 1889
Parents, Birth
and Early Childhood

The father, Hermann Kafka (1852–1931), who as a self-made man of his time spoke both German and Czech, came to Prague as a travelling merchant from the South Bohemian village of Osek. The poverty from which he stemmed and his difficult adolescence, as well as the psychological strain of establishing his business in Prague with insufficient capital, would later have consequences for the life and creative work of his son Franz, who was always confronted with the fate and abilities of his overpowering father.

The mother, Julie Kafka, née Löwy (1856–1934), was born in Poděbrady nad Labem. Julie was the daughter of a well-to-do brewery owner. Her mother died at the age of 28 of typhus. Julie viewed her happiness, above all, in the harmonious conformity to the wishes of her husband, whose views she increasingly shared out of selfless love and dependent obedience.

> My dear late husband was born in Wossek [Osek] near Strakonice. His father was a big, strong man. He was a butcher but did not reach an advanced age. His wife, my mother-in-law, had six children and was a delicate, industrious woman who raised her children well in spite of all the trouble and nuisance. They were her only happiness in life. My husband was sent abroad as a fourteen-year-old boy and had to support himself. In his twentieth year he became a soldier and later managed to become a train conductor. He married me when he was thirty. He had established himself with little means and, as we were both very industrious, became a respectable man. We had six children, of whom only three daughters are still alive. Our eldest son Franz was a delicate but healthy child. He

The parents: Hermann and Julie Kafka (around 1930)

was born in 1883. Two years later we had another boy, called Georg. He was a very strong, beautiful child who died of measles in his second year. Then came the third child. He passed away hardly six months of age because of an inflammation of the middle ear. His name was Heinrich. Our three daughters are happily married.

Julie Kafka

OLD TOWN SQUARE
(Staroměstské náměstí)

Kafka's life took place mainly in or around Old Town Square. The square, the centrepiece of Prague's Old Town, represents a unique ensemble of urban development. It appears much more spacious to the modern visitor than it did to Franz Kafka.

The Old Town Hall with its Apostle Clock (and neo-Gothic north wing still there at the turn of the century), the

Old Town Square: former marble fountain; in the background, the Týn Church (around 1860)

33

town residences, the Týn Church, the Church of St. Nicholas, the statue of Jan Hus, St. Mary's Column which dominated the square until 1918, Kinský Palace – all of these comprised the surroundings familiar to Franz Kafka.

Before her marriage, Kafka's mother lived in the Smetana House (Staroměstské náměstí 548/I). Adjacent to the Týn Church stood a café (Staroměstské nám. 549/I) which for a time was managed by Kafka's great-uncle Leopold. At the entrance to Celetná street, next to the Sixt House, described below, was the attorney's office of Dr. Richard Löwy, in which the newly graduated Franz Kafka would gather professional experience.

The following words, cited by his Hebrew teacher, Friedrich Thieberger, have since become famous:

> "Here was my secondary school, over there in that building facing us was the university, and a little further to the left, my office. My whole life" – and he drew a few small circles with his finger – "is confined to this small circle".

Franz Kafka to Friedrich Thieberger

In his diary, Franz Kafka described a dream in which Old Town Square forms the background for a theatrical scene:

Old Town Square: the Town Hall with the Apostle Clock (around 1895)

I dreamt the day before yesterday: all theatre, me once up in the gallery, once on stage, a girl I gladly would have had a few months ago acted in it, tensed her flexible body as, out of fear, she clung to the back of a chair; from the gallery I pointed at the girl, who played a breeches-part, my companion did not like her. In one act, the scenery was so big that you couldn't see anything else, no stage, no auditorium, no darkness, no footlights; instead, all the

Old Town Square: the Town Hall with the northern wing, which was destroyed in 1945 (around 1870)

spectators were in large numbers on the stage, which depicted Old Town Square, probably viewed from the end of Niklas Straße (Mikulášská). Nevertheless, although as a result one should not have been able to see the square in front of the Town Hall Clock and the Small Square [Malé náměstí], through short turns and slow swivels of the stage

Old Town Square: the southern side of the Town Hall decked out for the visit of Archduke Rudolf (1881)

35

Old Town Square: St. Nicholas Church; right, the no longer extant „Krenn House"

floor one could look over, for example, the Small Square from Kinský Palace. This had no purpose other than, possibly, to show all of the scenery, since it was already there in all its perfection and that it would have been a crying shame to miss any of the scenery, which, as I well knew, was the most beautiful scenery in the whole world and of all time. The lighting was defined by the dark, autumnal clouds. Light from the depressed sun gleamed diffusively in this or that painted window-pane on the southeastern side of the square. Since everything was realized in natural size and without revealing itself in the slightest, it made a moving impression that some of the open windows swung back and forth in the gentle wind, although because of the height of the buildings not a sound could be heard. The square sloped steeply, the cobblestones were black, the Týn Church was in its place, but in front of it stood a small imperial castle in whose forecourt were assembled, in perfect order, all of the monuments that usually stood on the square: St. Mary's Column, the old fountain in front of Town Hall, which I myself have never seen, the fountain in front of St. Nicholas Church, and a wooden fence which has been erected for the Hus Memorial.

Depicted was – in the auditorium it is often forgotten that one only depicts, just like first on the stage and in this scenery – an imperial festival and a revolution. The revolution was so great, with huge masses of people that were sent up and down the square, that it probably never took place in Prague; it was only moved to Prague because of the scenery, although it actually belonged in Paris. At first, nothing was seen of the festival, in any case the courtyard was laid out for the festival, in the meantime the revolution had broken out, the people had forced their way into the castle. I myself had just run across the projection of the fountain in the forecourt and into the open, returning to the castle, however, was impossible through the courtyards. Here came the court carriages from the Eisengasse [Železná] at such speed that they had to brake far from the castle entrance and ground across the cobblestones with locked wheels. They were carriages usually seen at fairs and processions on which living pictures had been placed, so they were flat, enveloped in a floral garland, and a colourful cloth hanging from the carriage board covered their wheels. One became increasingly aware of the terror that their speed signified. They were pulled in a curve from the Eisengasse to the castle by their horses, which reared up at the entrance, as if without awareness. Just then, a lot of people poured past me onto the square, mostly spectators whom I knew from the street and who had perhaps just arrived. Among them was a girl I knew, but I didn't know which one. Next to her walked an elegant young man with a yellowish-brown small-checked Ulster, his right hand buried in a pocket. They walked toward Niklas Straße. From that moment on, I saw nothing more.

from Franz Kafka's diaries (9. 11. 1911)

THE HOUSE OF KAFKA'S BIRTH
Mikulášská 9 (today: U radnice 5), Praha 1

Born on July 3, 1883, Franz Kafka was the first of six children born to the novelties merchant Hermann Kafka and his wife, Julie.

One week later, on July 10, in his parents' modest flat, Franz was circumcised according to tradition.

The house where Kafka was born was situated on the northeast side of Old Town Square (Conscription number 27/1), in the immediate vicinity of the Baroque Church of St. Nicholas, and lay on the edge of the Prague ghetto, still in existence at that time. The house was built between 1717 and 1730 by K. I. Dientzenhofer to serve as the prelate's office of St. Nicholas in the Old Town. After the dissolution of the monastery in 1787 by Josef II, the building was used as a residential house.

The Kafka family lived in this house only until May. In endeavouring to improve their standard of living, the Kafkas, and with them little Franz, moved several times in the space of a few years. Thus, between 1885 and 1888 they lived succes-

The house in which Franz Kafka was born (around 1898)

The memorial plaque on the house in which Kafka was born

sively on Wenceslas Square, in Dušní street and in Pařižská street.

It is obvious that this lack of constancy would affect the child's development. In addition, his mother had to return to work soon after Franz's birth and often left him alone or in the care of a wet-nurse.

After it burned down in 1887, a new building (erected 1902, architect R. Kříženecký) replaced the house in which Franz Kafka was born and of which only the portal remained. Today the building houses a small, permanent Franz Kafka exhibition.

In 1965 a bust by Karel Hladík was mounted onto the building's exterior wall in commemoration of Kafka. In anticipation of Prague Spring, Kafka had finally become acceptable to the communist regime as a "revolutionary critic of capitalist alienation".

THE SIXT HOUSE
Celetná 2, Praha 1

Between August 1888 and May 1889 the Kafka family lived in the so-called Sixt House in Celetná 2. The building is named after the aristocratic family of Sixt von Ottersdorf, who owned the building in the sixteenth and seventeenth centuries. The building has the date 1796 engraved above the door, though it is much older, for it has cross- and barrel-vaulting dating from the 1220s.

This building saw such illustrious personalities as Cola da Rienzi, Francesco Petrarca and Johannes Faust as its temporary occupants. It later belonged to Philipp Fabricus, the scribe who, in 1618, was thrown out of the window of the Chancellery of Bohemia in the Prague Castle. Fabricus survived the defenestration, upon which the Emperor bestowed on him the title "von Hohenfall" (fallen from on high).

Old Town Square (south side) and Celetná street around 1870: the Sixt House (fifth building from the right)

HERMANN KAFKA'S FIRST SHOP
"Hotel Goldhammer"
Staroměstské náměstí 12 (today 8), Praha 1

In 1882, the year of his marriage to Julie Löwy and a year before the birth of Franz, Hermann Kafka's novelty shop was established first in retail, later wholesale, as "Hermann Kafka's
Fashion Accessories". The first commercial building, the
"Hotel Goldhammer" on the north side of Old Town Square,
has not been preserved. Franz Kafka writes about the shop:

> Actually, especially in my childhood, as long as it was still
> a small, simple shop, I ought to have liked it very much,
> it was so lively, lit up in the evening there was so much to
> see and to hear, one could help here and there and dis-
> tinguish oneself, but above all admire you with your
> magnificent commercial talents, how you sold things,
> dealt with people, joked, were untiring, in cases of doubt
> at once knew the right decision, and so on; even the way

Old Town Square: View of the north side, with the Hotel Goldhammer
(around 1898)

41

you wrapped a parcel or unpacked a crate was a sight worth seeing, the whole of it all in all not the worst schooling for a child. But since you gradually began to terrify me on all sides, and the shop and you became inseparable for me, the shop was no longer a pleasant place for me to be. Things which had at first been a matter of course for me began to torment and shame me, especially your treatment of the staff. I don't know, perhaps this was the case in most shops (at Assicurazioni Generali, for example, in my time it was really similar, I explained my resignation to the director there, not quite truthfully but not entirely a lie either, by the fact that I could not stand the cursing, which, incidentally, had not even been meant for me directly; I was too painfully sensitive to this from home), but the other shops did not concern me during my childhood. But you I heard and saw screaming, cursing and raging in the shop, in a manner that, in my opinion at the time, had no equal anywhere in the world. And not only abuse, but other tyrannies, too. For example, the way you jerked goods down off the counter that you did not want to have mixed up with the other things – only the blindness of your rage excused you a little – and how the sales clerk had to pick them up. Or your constant comments about a sales clerk suffering from tuberculosis: "Let him croak, the sick dog." You called your employees "paid enemies", and this they were, but even before they became that, you seemed to me to be their "paying enemy". There, too, I learned the great lesson that you could be unjust; in my case I would not have noticed it so soon for I had accumulated too many feelings of guilt, which made me ready to agree with you; but in my childish opinion – later, of course, somewhat modified, although not all too much so – there were strangers in the shop who nevertheless worked for us, and because of this had to live in perpetual fear of you.

Franz Kafka, Letter to his father

However, *Letter to his father*, which Kafka wrote in his later years and never delivered, is not the only source the often ailing son left behind regarding his father, who was bursting with health and vitality. Most of the remarks he noted in his diaries also testify to the fact that the relationship between the son and his father was difficult:

> It is unpleasant to listen when Father, with incessant side-swipes at the fortunate circumstances of his contemporaries and, above all, his children, recounts the sufferings he had to endure in his youth. No one denies that, because of insufficient winter clothing, he had open wounds on his legs for years, that he often went hungry, that already at the age of 10 he had to pull a small wagon through the villages even in winter and very early in the morning – but these true facts, in regard to the other true fact that I did not suffer any of that, do not in the least lead to the conclusion that I have been happier than he was, that he can be arrogant because of these wounds on his legs, that he from the very beginning assumes and maintains that I am not able to respect his early sufferings and that I, especially because I have not suffered equally, must show boundless gratitude to him. How gladly I would listen if he ceaselessly talked about his youth and his parents, but to listen to all of it in that boasting and scolding tone is torture. Again and again he slaps his hands together: "Who knows this today? What do the children know? No one has suffered this! Does any child understand this today?" Today he spoke like this to Aunt Julie, who is visiting. She also possesses the enormous face that all relatives on Father's side have. The eyes are very slightly and disturbingly badly embedded or coloured. At 10, she was hired out as a cook. She had to fetch things in bitter cold while wearing a wet skirt. The skin on her legs cracked, the skirt froze and did not dry until night, in bed.
>
> from Franz Kafka's diaries (26. 12. 1911)

43

Funeral procession through the Prague New Town on the occasion of the burial of the writer Jan Neruda (1891)

1889 – 1893
ATTENDING ELEMENTARY SCHOOL
AT THE FLEISCHMARKT (MASNÝ TRH)

THE HOUSE "U MINUTY"
(AT THE MINUTE)
Staroměstské náměstí 2, Praha 1

Between June 1889 and September 1896, the Kafka family lived in this house, which dates from the seventeenth century. Franz's three sisters, Elli, Valli and Ottla, were born here. All three would later perish in Nazi concentration camps.

The house with its sgraffito (which were painted over during Kafka's time) brings to mind the Schwarzenberg Palace at Hradčany.

The sgraffito were applied around 1615 and depict biblical and classical myths and legends.

The watchful lion on the ceiling, who holds a cartouche in its front paws, is a vestige of the chemist's "Zum Weißen Löwen" (At the White Lion) which was once housed here and was outfitted by a certain Mathias Bartl after he had bought the house in 1712. The chemist's closed its doors in 1850, after over 130 years of operation. A tobacconist's was housed here before the turn of the century, when the Kafka family lived in the buil-  ding. The access gallery

The house At the Minute on Old Town Square

Arcade on Old Town Square

around the building did not exist during Kafka's lifetime; it was first opened in 1938.

Decades later, Kafka recounted an incident from his childhood to his friend Milena Jesenská:

Once as a small boy, I'd received a sixpence and wanted very much to give it to an old beggar woman who was sitting between Old Town Square and Small Square. Now, this seemed to me an outrageous sum, a sum which most likely had never been given a beggar before, and I felt embarrassed in front of the woman to be doing something so outrageous, so I changed the sixpence and gave the woman a penny, walked around the entire complex of the Town Hall and the arcade along the Small Square, reappeared from the left as a completely new do-gooder, gave the woman another penny, started again to walk and happily did this ten times (or perhaps a little less, for I believe the woman later lost patience and left). In any case, in the end I was so exhausted, morally too, that I went home right away and cried until my mother replaced the sixpence.

Franz Kafka to Milena Jesenská (1920)

From this house little Franz also set out on his first journey to school.

In another letter to Jesenská we discover details of the regular morning walk to Fleischmarktgasse (Masná) 16 (today No. 6), where the German Elementary School for Boys in Old Prague was located. The house is now used as a residental building:

Our cook, a small, dry, skinny, sharp-nosed, hollow-cheeked, yellowish yet firm, energetic and superior woman, led me to school each morning. We lived in the house which separates Small Square from Old Town Square. First, we would walk across the square, then into the Teingasse [Týnská], then through a sort of archway into Fleischmarktgasse and down to the Fleischmarkt. And now the same thing was repeated every morning for perhaps a year. Upon leaving the house the cook would say that she was going to tell the teacher how bad I'd been at home. Now, I was probably not so very bad, but obstinate, good-for-nothing, sad and naughty, things which could most certainly be made up into a charming tale for the teacher. This I knew and so I did not take the cook's threats lightly. However, I believed the walk to school to be so tremendously long, and plenty could still happen (out of such childish thoughtlessness a fear and dead-eyed seriousness gradually developed, since the streets are not really so terribly long). I was also very much in doubt, at least while still in Old Town Square, as to whether the cook, who was after all an authority figure, though only a domestic one, would really dare to speak to the teacher, a person of world authority.

Charles Bridge after its collapse (1890)

Franz Kafka during his first year at secondary school

Perhaps I would even say as much, then the cook would answer shortly, with her thin merciless lips, that I didn't have to believe her, but say it she would. About the time we were to turn into Fleischmarktgasse – it still has some small historic significance for me (in which neighbourhood did you live as a child?) – the fear of this threat became predominant. School itself was already a horror, and now the cook wanted to make it even more difficult for me. I would begin to plead, she would shake her head; the more I pleaded, the more I felt what I was pleading for to be of value, the greater the danger; I would stand still and beg for forgiveness, she dragged me along; I would threaten her with retaliation through my parents, she laughed, here she was almighty; I held onto the doorframes of the shops, onto the cornerstones, I didn't want to go on until she had forgiven me, I tore her back by her skirt (she didn't have it easy either), but she dragged me further, assuring me that even this she was going to report to the teacher; it would get late, the clock of the Church of St. James struck 8:00, you could hear the schoolbells, other children began to run, I was always most afraid of being late, by now we would have to run as well and always the thought, "She's going to tell, she's not going to tell"; as it happened, she did not tell, ever, but she always had the opportunity, and a seemingly increasing one (yesterday I did not tell, but today I will for sure), and from that she never desisted. And sometimes – think of it, Milena – she would stamp her feet in anger at me in the lane and a coal merchant was sometimes around and she would watch us. Milena, what foolishness, and how I belong to you with all the cooks and threats and all that enormous amount of dust that 38 years has whirled up and which has settled in my lungs.

Franz Kafka to Milena Jesenská (1920)

As children we lived near to one another and took the same route to our elementary school at the Fleischmarkt. When we, coming from the neighbourhood of the Týn Church, went to school, we first had to pass the many meat shops of the market. Across from the meat shops

49

was the Czech school, a rival of our German school. At the entrance to the rival school a bust of the great Czech pedagogue Komenský was displayed, and under it his words in Czech: "A Czech child belongs in a Czech school!" These words were meant here as a warning to Czech parents who brought their children to the German schools. But were we Czech children? Whether we knew it or not, we carried the thousand-year-old heritage and destiny of a folk which was used to living between other folk.

Hugo Bergmann

As the family of the businessman Hermann Kafka did not belong to the traditionally educated middle-class, Franz was at a disadvantage compared to others his age. His future friend Max Brod had the opportunity to read the works of Shakespeare, Goethe, Schiller etc. in the collection in his father's library. Franz's parents had difficulty understanding his reading habits and his attempts at writing; they would have preferred to see Franz develop interest in his father's business, which he was supposed to take over one day.

Advert in Prager Tagblatt (around 1900)

And particularly because of this business, the parents had little time for the needs of their growing son. Therefore, employees of the family, such as the cook, described earlier, the housekeeper Marie Werner or the French governess Bailly, had to substitute for them in raising the young boy.

Prague pretzel salesman

Prague street scene (1897)

1893 – 1901
SECONDARY SCHOOL

THE IMPERIAL AND ROYAL OLD TOWN GERMAN
SECONDARY SCHOOL IN THE KINSKÝ PALACE
Staroměstské náměstí 12, Praha 1

Beginning September 1891 Kafka attended this humanist,
state-run German-language secondary school in Old Town
Square. He finally graduated from this institution, housed in
the back of the Kinský Palace, in summer of 1901, even
though he constantly feared

> ... that I will not pass this year's final examinations, and
> that, if I should succeed I will not get along in the next
> year, and even if this could be avoided by cheating, that
> I will finally fail at the school-leaving exam, and by the
> way, that I, irrespective of the moment, will surprise my
> parents as well as the rest of the world – made sleepy by
> my apparently orderly progress – by the sudden revela-
> tion of my scandalous inability.
> from Franz Kafka's diaries (2. 1. 1912)

Kafka was quite a good pupil, a first-rate student in the first
three years, according to the school's yearly report. In spite of
private tutoring, however, he was constantly at loggerheads
with mathematics.

The humanist education that Kafka received should not be
measured in every detail by modern educational standards.
Even so, attendance at this particularly strict secondary
school greatly increased the chances of gaining work in the
hierarchy of the imperial and royal civil service. Thus, surely
not without good reason, Kafka's father had purposefully

chosen precisely this school for his son. The institution was supposed to introduce the students, e.g. by cramming Latin and Greek, to the Classical world and spirit. But the reality was very different.

If, in Kafka's case, conditions were different, it is still interesting to read the related school experiences of another Prague student, the Bohemian writer and philosopher Fritz Mauthner, who was born in the small town of Hořice in 1849:

> Among us students – we were now about forty in the class – only three or four were so stimulated that they were able, with difficulty, to translate an old classic word for word; the stereotyped enthusiasm for Homer and Sophocles was not lacking among these chosen ones either; but there was an utter lack of understanding for the special way, the incomparability and inimitability, and thus also for the foreignness, of the Classical spirit. And the other pupils, nine-tenths of the class, even passed the school-leaving exams successfully, without knowing anything about the Classical languages but the cane. They derived neither enjoyment nor use from the Classical languages and learned a few passages only to forget them again immediately following the exams.
>
> Fritz Mauthner

The German lessons that Kafka received acquainted him with authors who were considered important by the educated classes at the turn of the century. Nonetheless, in his lessons Kafka also got to know such prominent writers as Johann Peter Hebel, whose *Schatzkästlein des rheinischen Hausfreundes* (Jewellery Box of the Rhenish Friend of the Family) was to become one of Kafka's favourite books; in addition, the curriculum included Grillparzer, Eichendorff, Kleist, Stifter, and of course Goethe and Schiller.

Kafka must have familiarized himself with German fairy tales as well as Classical material – which later appeared in his work – through school readers and his teachers.

The Kinský Palace, one of the most beautiful of Prague's palaces, is a mature work of Kilian Ignaz Dientzenhofer, executed by Anselmo Lurago (1755–1765). The sculptured decoration of the palace was produced in the workshop of Ignaz Platzer.

Nobel Price-winner Bertha von Suttner ("Die Waffen nieder" – Down with the weapons), born in 1843, spent the first years of her childhood in the Kinský Palace.

On February 1948, communist Prime Minister Klement Gottwald announced from the balcony of the palace, which was no longer in the possession of the Kinský family, the dismissal of the bourgeois ministers.

Today, the building, with its unique rococo façade jutting out onto Old Town Square, houses a collection of paintings from the National Gallery.

The inner court, where the school was situated, is no longer accessible. Hermann Kafka's flourishing business was temporarily (1912–1918) located in this palace. Today the name of a bookstore, housed on the premises of the former paternal business since 1995, recalls this.

Kinský Palace on Old Town Square

The House "At the Three Kings"
Celetná 3, Praha 1

In 1896 the Kafkas moved into the first floor of the late Gothic house "At the Three Kings". Franz Kafka, who had just entered the fourth year of secondary school, was to continue living in this house throughout the rest of his school years until his graduation, and also during his years of university study and his year in court.

Franz, who at this time had to deal with the worries and anxieties of puberty, had his own single room and could look directly onto the lively Celetná Street.

> Whoever leads a lonesome life and yet every so often would like to have some kind of contact, whoever wants, considering the changes in the time of day, the weather, the state of his business and such, just to have an arm he might cling to within sight, such a person will not carry on long without a window on the street. And if it is the case that he is not looking for anything at all and merely steps to the windowsill a weary man, letting his eyes wander up and down between the public and the sky, and is reluctant to look and has tilted his head slightly back, even then the horses below him will tear him away into their train of wagons and noise and thus at last into human harmony.
>
> Franz Kafka,
> "The Window
> onto the Street",
> in *Meditation*

Portal of the house Celetná No. 3

"The Window onto the Street" is one of Kafka's earliest works. He later destroyed almost all other works from his school years he had begun writing in 1897. "The Window onto the Street" was later included in his first book *Meditation*. In addition to several texts for *Meditation*, the first draft of "Description of a Struggle" was also written in this house.

The following extant reports of a domestic employee and Kafka's schoolmate Hugo Bergmann convey an impression of Franz's room in the house "At the Three Kings" during his years of study:

> His room was simply furnished. Beside the door was a desk and on it lay the *Roman Law* in two volumes. Opposite the window was a wardrobe, in front of it a bicycle, then the bed, beside the bed a night table, and at the door there was a bookshelf and a sink.
>
> Anna Pouzarová

> We both became friends from early youth. Franz's mother knew my mother, and so I soon became a fellow tenant of Franz's in their house in Zeltnergasse. It made a great impression on me that Franz already had his own room as a young pupil, from which one could look down upon Zeltnergasse; indeed, that he even owned his own desk.
>
> Hugo Bergmann

In September 1886 his father's shop was also moved to Celetná 3. Hermann Kafka advanced to the position of "certified expert" of the imperial and royal court of trade, and his retail business went wholesale. Kafka could muster little interest in this. A university course of study was more interesting for him because it delayed his definitive entry into the business world and promised more time for writing.

Bridge consecration by Emperor Franz Joseph (1901)

1901
The Commencement of Kafka's Studies at the German University in Prague

After graduating from Gymnasium (secondary school) and a week of holiday on Norderney and Helgoland, Franz's student years at Prague University began.

The long-established Charles University had, as of 1882, been split into a German and a Czech university. Franz Kafka registered at the German university for the winter semester of 1901–1902. After a two-week attempt at studying chemistry and a brief intermission in German studies (with the legendary German scholar August Sauer) Kafka remained at the Faculty of Law until he finished his doctorate. The law students were accommodated in the Carolinum (enter from Železná) but they also studied at the jurisprudence department (Ovocný trh 5) and at the political science department (Husova 20, Clam-Gallas Palace). Another one of Kafka's places of study was the five-courtyard-long former Jesuit college Clementinum, in which he attended lectures in German literature, art history and philosophy and borrowed books from the university library.

Franz Kafka's academic achievements were rather mediocre. The study of law was for him a kind of stopgap; after all, as a Jew, he had to take a pragmatic approach:

> For a Jew who had completed university studies and did not want to be baptised in order to pursue a career as a civil servant, there were, under the circumstances of the time, virtually only the 'free' professions to choose from: law and medicine.
>
> Hugo Bergmann

So there was no real freedom in the choice of profession for me, I knew: in consideration of the main thing I would be just as indifferent to everything else as I had been to all the subjects at secondary school, so it was a matter of finding a profession that would most likely allow me to indulge this indifference without injuring my vanity all too much. Therefore, law was the obvious choice. Small, contrary attempts on the part of vanity, of senseless hope, such as a fourteen-day study of chemistry or a half-year of German studies, only strengthened that fundamental conviction. So I studied law. This meant that in the few months before the exams, in a way that severely tested my nerves, I literally nourished myself, intellectually speaking, on sawdust that had, moreover, already been chewed by a thousand mouths. But in a certain sense this was exactly to my taste, as in a certain sense the secondary school had been earlier and later my job as a clerk, for it all completely suited my situation.

Franz Kafka, Letter to his father

THE CAROLINUM
Železna 9, Praha 1

Charles University was founded April 7, 1348, as the first central European university and moved its quarters in 1383 into the house of the royal mintmaster Johann Rotlöw, not far from Old Town Square. Only a magnificent Gothic oriel as part of the chapel of saints Cosmas and Damian (about 1370), an arcade and the great hall on the second floor in which academic ceremonies are still held today, recall the beginnings of this important school, which over the centuries became the mirror of Bohemian history.

Gothic oriel on the Carolinum

Following the university's early hey-day, at the beginning of the century, the Kuttenberg Decree of 1409, in which King Wenceslas IV submitted to the demands of Rector Jan Hus after the Bohemian nation's struggle for superiority in the university's self-government, brought about the school's decline.

The "natio Bohemica", to which both the German and Czech citizens of the Bohemian crownlands belonged, now had three votes in the uni-

Atalantes on the portal to the Clam-Gallas Palace

versity's self-governance, while the Bavarian, Saxon and Polish university nations had to be satisfied with one vote each.

A huge number of students and university teachers and professors then left the Charles University staff to study at other universities (Cracow, Heidelberg, Vienna, Cologne; in Leipzig, a new university was even founded). Charles University was known as a heretics' nest until it was taken over by the Jesuits in 1622. In the 19th and 20th centuries, the college was also the scene of nationalistic and political disputes, which manifested themselves in its division.

On November 17, 1939, the Czech university was closed on orders of the head of the Reichsprotektorat. In 1945, President Beneš exacted some measure of revenge by retroactively closing the German university. Charles University was to play an important role in the nation's political history two more times: in 1967–68, at the time of the so-called Prague Spring, and in 1989, when its student body, 50 years to the day after the Czech university was closed by the German occupiers, played no small role in the Velvet Revolution.

View of Vltava bridges from Letná

1902 – 1903
FRANZ KAFKA AND MAX BROD
BECOME ACQUAINTED

> For you know, Max, my love for you is greater than me,
> and more inhabited by me than that it lives in me, and it
> also has a weak hold on my insecure being.
> > Franz Kafka to Max Brod (1908)

Franz Kafka is described as a reserved yet sociable person with
a sense of humour, who certainly knew how to make friends
and valued friendship. He not only attended cultural events,
lectures and the like with his friends; they also amused themselves, as is the habit of students (and perhaps necessary for
maturity), in cafés, at variety shows, in pubs, bars and, later
on, brothels.

Names that sounded melodious to Prague's bohemians –
Salon Goldschmidt ("Gogo"), Trocadéro, Eldorado, Lucerna
or London – also became the epitomes of nocturnal amusement for the young Kafka. The zest for life that he expressed
in adventures of this kind stands in blatant contradiction to
the black-and white image that has been created over the
years.

> My dear Max,
> When are we going to the Indian dancer, since after all
> the little miss has run away from us, and whose aunt is at
> the moment still stronger than her talent. Franz
> > Franz Kafka to Max Brod (1906)

Max Brod

My dear Max,

Instead of our planned nightlife from Monday to Tuesday, we could organize a nice little morning life, we could meet at 5 o'clock or 5:30 at St. Mary's Column – we wouldn't be short of women then – and go to the Trocadero or to Kuchelbad or to the Eldorado. Then we could, as it suits us, drink coffee in the garden on the Vltava or lean on the shoulder of Joszi. Both are praiseworthy. Because in the Trocadero, we wouldn't suffer much; there are millionaires and even richer folk who have no money left at six in the morning and, robbed of everything at all the other wine bars, we would now, unfortunately, die in the last one because we need to drink a small coffee and only because we were millionaires – or we still are, who knows that in the morning – are we able to pay for a second little cup.

Franz Kafka to Max Brod (1908)

Evenings, nights of this blessed winter! How we were one, how we were in tune there. We sat in the cafés, we rollicked through the nocturnal city, we climbed up the awkward Hradčany, we roamed along the wide river.

Otto Pick

Despite all the joys of a student's life, the 20–year-old Kafka observed the political and social goings-on with keen interest. In a letter to Oskar Pollak, for example, Kafka reported, with sympathy, about the protest marches of the commercial employees, who were struggling for their social rights:

Today is Sunday, and still the commercial employees come down Wenceslas Square, across the Graben, and clamour for a day of rest on Sunday [Na Příkopě]. I think their red carnations and their foolish and Jewish faces and their shouting is something very sensible. It is almost as if a child wanted to go to Heaven and howls and barks because no one will hand him a stool. But he doesn't really want to go to Heaven. The others, however, who are walking on the Graben and smile at it because they themselves don't know what to do with their Sundays,

I'd slap them if I had the courage for it and were not
smiling myself.

Franz Kafka to Oskar Pollak (1903)

Until around 1903, Kafka's talented schoolmate Oskar Pollak
was one of his closest friends; thereafter his lifelong friendship
with Max Brod, one year his junior, gradually became the decisive relationship. Franz, who spent his first university holidays visiting his uncle, the country doctor Siegfried Löwy, in
Triesch, first spoke to Max Brod on October 23, 1902, after a
lecture in the German Students' Reading and Lecture Hall.
Brod had presented a paper on "Fates and Future in Scho-
penhauer's Philosophy" and thereby set Kafka, a convinced
follower of Nietzsche, a few questions to think about.

> I got to know Franz Kafka during my first year at uni-
> versity, in 1902–03, presumably already in the winter se-
> mester of 1902. Franz, about a year older than me, was
> already in his third semester. After leaving secondary
> school he had first enrolled in chemistry for fourteen
> days, then for a semester in German Studies, then law,
> the last only as a stopgap without any predilection for it,
> like so many of us. The study of law, as the most uncer-
> tain of studies, encompassing no goals or the largest
> number of goals (advocating, the civil service), the deci-
> sion for a career which did not require any special
> predilection and was forever put off, was taken up with a
> sigh.
>
> Max Brod, *About Franz Kafka*

THE FORMER GERMAN STUDENTS' READING AND DISCUSSION HALL

The German Students' Reading and Discussion Hall in
Prague, which until 1904 was housed in Ferdinand Straße
(today Národní) 12 and thereafter in Krakovská 14, would
come to play a major role in Kafka's intellectual development.
One simply spoke of 'the Hall' in student circles when speak-

ing of this umbrella organisation of Prague's liberal German-speaking students. Kafka took part in the literary and social events, and as of the winter semester of 1903 he also took over the function of art correspondent and, later, literary correspondent.

Brod gives an account of their first meeting in "the Hall":

> The place of our first encounter was the German Students' Reading- and Discussion-Hall. ... The literary "Section" had its regular debating and internal lecture evenings. On one of these evenings I made my debut, fresh out of secondary school, with a lecture "Schopenhauer and Nietzsche", which caused a sensation because I, the bitter and fanatical Schopenhaueran that I was in those days, and one who took the slightest contradiction of the theses of my idolized philosopher as a lése majesté, had spoken of Nietzsche quite simply and bluntly as a "swindler"...
>
> After this lecture Kafka, who was one year older than me, accompanied me home. He used to take part in all the meetings of the "Section" but up until that time we had hardly taken notice of one another. And it would have been difficult to notice him, who so seldom took the floor and whose external nature was a profound unobtrusivenes even his elegant, usually dark blue suits were as inconspicuous and reserved as he himself. But this time something about me seemed to have attracted him; he was more open than usual. However, the never-ending discussion accompanying our way home began with a strong contradiction of my all-too-crude formulations.
>
> Max Brod, *About Franz Kafka*

In place of the building of the former German Students' Reading and Lecture Hall in Národní třída, there is today an unsightly vacant lot, and nothing now recalls the once so important institution.

THE CAFÉ LOUVRE
Národní třída 20, Praha 1

The Café Louvre

Kafka, along with his friends Max Brod, Hugo Bergmann and Felix Weltsch, belonged to a philosophic circle that met at the Café Louvre. The circle devoted most of its time to the teachings of the philosopher Franz Brentano, then very influential in Prague. The visits to the Café Louvre ended in 1905 because Max Brod, who had spoken disparagingly of the master in his book *Twins of the Soul*, was expelled from the circle.

THE SALON OF BERTA FANTA
(HOUSE "AT THE UNICORN")
Staroměstské náměstí 18, Praha 1

Franz Kafka, still a student, also took part, as a silent listener, in the private discussions held at the home of the ambitious Berta Fanta, a pharmacist's wife who played an important role in Prague's cultural life and whose daughter Else married Kafka's schoolmate and friend Hugo Bergmann in 1908. Although the participants in these discussions tended to follow the world-view of the Brentanists, the basic works of Fichte, Kant and Hegel, among other philosophers, were also read and discussed.

> Incidentally, Kafka had an effect not only on me, but on many in the already mentioned trend. Within this circle and under the hospitality of Frau Berta Fanta where,

under the enthusiastic participation of the hostess, exacting philosophy was studied, Kafka was held in high esteem, simply because of his personality, his occasional comments, and his conversation, for at the time nobody but me knew his literary works.

Max Brod, *About Franz Kafka*

However, Berta Fanta and the circle gathered around her did not only discuss conventional philosophy, but also occupied themselves with all the esoteric doctrines that fascinated Prague society at the time: spiritualism, the teachings of the Indian sages, the esoteric teachings of Helena Blavatsky and, of course, Rudolf Steiner's Theosophist movement with all its occult concepts about physiological processes and laws. Not only Gustav Meyrink, who was always open to such theories, but also Franz Werfel, Willy Haas, Max Brod, Franz Kafka and many others interested themselves in this spiritual hodge-podge. However, Kafka – who in many respects had a very individualistic stance toward science – maintained a skeptical distance.

That the sun will rise tomorrow morning is a miracle ..., but that a table moves when you maltreat it for so long, that is no wonder.

Franz Kafka to Willy Haas

The house „At the Unicorn" (second from left) on Old Town Square

Fair outside Prague; left, the Petřín with the Hunger Wall (around 1880).

My Visit to Dr. Steiner:

A woman is already waiting (upstairs in the second floor of the Viktoria Hotel in Jungmannova), but she urges me to enter before her. We wait. The secretary comes and asks us to wait. Looking down the corridor, I see him. Immediately thereafter he comes toward us with half-outstreched arms. The woman explains that I was there first. I now walk behind him as he leads me to his room... In his room, I look for my humility, which I cannot feel, by asking to be shown a ridiculous place to put my hat; I put it on a small wooden stand used to tie one's boots... He listened very attentively without apparently observing me in the least, totally concentrated upon my words. From time to time he nodded, which he seemingly takes for an aid to intense concentration. At the beginning, he was annoyed by a mild cold, it ran out of his nose, he constantly worked his handkerchief deep into his nose, one finger in each nostril.

From Franz Kafka's diaries, 28. 3. 1911

Collecting ice from the frozen Vltava (1900)

Frau Fanta saw to it that only select individuals set the tone, so that after the events ended, the fresh air of Old Town Square was just as welcome as it was necessary. Kafka was mostly just a quiet listener, occasionally he would throw in a relevant question or a sharp comment which brought the "elevated" discussion back down to earth. Now and again he stayed away from the meetings, repelled by the arrogant manner in which these evenings had developed. I think it was on an evening in 1913 that the German poet Else Lasker-Schüler was the guest of honour. She had a very affected and exaggerated way about her. We left the event towards midnight (I remember that Franz Werfel and Egon Erwin Kisch were also present), and our visitor – she called herself "Prince of Thebes' and tried hard to look the part, too – sank onto her knees facing the beautiful square, whose Gothic towers left and right were bathed in almost supernatural moonlight, and began to recite an improvised ode. A policeman intervened and asked who she was. She replied proudly, "I am the prince of Thebes". Whereupon Kafka corrected her, "She is not the prince of Thebes, but a cow [Ger: *Kuh*] from the Kurfürstendamm".

Leopold Kreitner

Now 20 years old, Kafka began to have his first sexual experiences.

In a letter to Milena Jesenská, he described an experience from the time he was just preparing for his exam in the history of law:

> We were living in Zeltnergasse at that time. Opposite was a clothes shop, a shopgirl was always standing in the doorway. I was a little over the age of 20, ceaselessly pacing back and forth in my room, preoccupied with the nerve-racking rote-learning of what I considered to be senseless things for the first state exam. It was summer, very hot at this time I guess, it was absolutely unbearable, at the window I remained, the disgusting Roman Law History between my teeth, always standing. Finally, we communicated through signs. I was to fetch her at eight o'clock in the evening, but when I went down, another

was already there, well, that did not change a lot, I was afraid of the entire world, and also of this man; had he not been there, I would still have been afraid of him. But though the girl slipped her arm through his, she gave me a sign that I should follow them. Thus we came to the Schützeninsel, drank beer there, I at the neighbouring table, then we slowly walked, with me behind, to the girl's flat, somewhere around the Fleischmarkt. There the man took his leave, the girl disappeared into the house, I waited for a bit until she came out again, and then we went to a hotel on the Kleinseite. All that was charming, exciting and disgusting, even before the hotel, and in the hotel it was no different.

And when, towards morning, it was still hot and beautiful, we went back home over the Charles Bridge, I was, of course, happy, but this happiness meant only that my eternally moaning body had finally found relief, but most of all, this happiness consisted of the fact that the whole thing had not been even more disgusting, even dirtier. When I was together with the girl once more, two nights later, I think, everything was as good as the first time, but then when I went away on summer holidays, and played a bit with a girl outside, I could not look at the shopgirl in Prague again.

Franz Kafka to Milena Jesenská (1920)

Interior of a Prague café

1904 – 1905
BEGINNING WORK ON
"DESCRIPTION OF A STRUGGLE"

> A book must be the axe for the frozen sea within us. I be-
> lieve that.
>
> Franz Kafka to Oskar Pollak (1904)

In the winter semester of 1904–1905, 21–year-old Franz
Kafka started work on the first version of his visionary narra-
tive "Description of a Struggle", in which the I-narrator describes a nocturnal walk – with an antagonist recognizable as
Kafka's fellow student Ewald Přibram – through wintry, de-
serted Prague. The intensely dream-like plot has autobio-
graphical aspects. In none other of Kafka's preserved works
does Prague play such a central role. Many of the places and
monuments mentioned by Kafka – some of which will be introduced in the following pages – present themselves virtually
unchanged to the modern viewer; a few, like St. Mary's Column in Old Town Square, have fallen victim to the folly of
the revolutionary Zeitgeist of our century.

ST. MARY'S COLUMN
IN OLD TOWN SQUARE
(Staroměstské náměstí)

> In 1650 Emperor Ferdinand III had the still standing St.
> Mary's Column, a monolith with a statue of the
> Immaculate Conception, erected by the royal sculptor,
> Georg Pendel, as a sign of gratitude for the deliverance
> from the Swedes, who in vain besieged the town below
> Königsmark in 1648. The astronomer David had it set
> up in 1825 as a midday indicator by having its shadow

View of the northern side of Old Town Square with St. Mary's Column (around 1870)

fall upon the stone stripe which lies on the side of the Kinský Palace at exactly midday.

Griebens Reiseführer Prag, 1911

If one builds such large squares only out of arrogance, why not also build a stone railing that could lead through the square. Today a southwest wind is blowing. The air in the square is agitated. The tip of the Town Hall tower describes small circles. Why don't they pipe down in this crush? What noise! All the window-panes are kicking up a row and the lampposts are bending like bamboo. The coat of St. Mary on the column bulges outward and the stormy wind tears at it. Does no one see it? The ladies and gentlemen, who should be walking on the stones, are floating. When the wind draws breath, they stop, say a few words to one another and bow in greeting, but when the wind pushes again, they cannot resist it and they all lift their feet simultaneously. Although they have to hold on to their hats, there is amusement in their eyes, as if the weather were mild. Only I am afraid.

Franz Kafka, Description of a Struggle

St. Mary's Column, which was toppled in 1918 by the revolutionary mob in front of the Town Hall, and at whose base an oil lamp constantly burned, was during Kafka's youth a site for devout meditation and celebration of the Virgin Mary. For Kafka it was also a place at which he arranged to meet his friend Max Brod:

> Dear Max, you know I have work, thus a new year has begun and my sufferings, provided that thus far they've been walking on foot, are now correspondingly walking on their hands. I'd like very much to meet you at 2:30 at St. Mary's Column in the square, on time, please, if possible. Yours, Franz K.
>
> Franz Kafka to Max Brod (1908)

THE WELL IN THE SMALL SQUARE
(Malé náměstí)

> As I passed by the fire station I heard a noise from the Small Square, and when I entered it I saw a drunk standing by the iron grille of the well ...
>
> Franz Kafka,
> *Description
> of a Struggle*

From Old Town Square you reach the Small Square [Malé náměstí] to the west, which has preserved its historic character to an even greater extent. In the centre stands a well with an ironwork grille from the year 1560.

*Griebens Reiseführer
Prag*, 1911

Fountain in the Small Square (Malé náměstí)

THE OLD TOWN MILL TOWER
Novotného lávka

> He obviously told the time from the clock of the Mill
> Tower.
>
> Franz Kafka, *Description of a Struggle*

> Passing the Bellevue Café, a beautiful new building in
> Dutch Renaissance style, one reaches the picturesquely
> situated Old Town mills. Here is a water tower built as
> early as 1489 which has been destroyed seven times by
> fire as well as during the Swedish siege. The height of the
> tower, newly erected in 1878, is 53 m. Next to it is the
> municipal water office, built in 1883 in Renaissance
> style with sgraffitos by Aleš and Ženíšek, which refer to
> the time of the Swedes.
>
> *Griebens Reiseführer Prag,* 1911

Novotného lávka with Old Town Mill Tower

Kreuzherrenplatz (Křižovnické náměstí) and Karlsgasse
(Karlova)

But now I knew what I had to do, because right before horrible events I am possessed with great determination. I had to run away. It was very simple. Now on the left the turning onto Charles Bridge, I could jump to the right into Karlsgasse. It was winding, there were dark doorways and still open taverns; there was no need for me to despair.

When we emerged from under the arch at the end of the quay, I ran into the street with my arms raised; but just as I reached the small door of the church, I fell, for there was a step I had not seen. There was a crashing sound. The next streetlight was some distance away; I lay in the darkness. From a tavern opposite [the former wine bar U Kosků, Karlová 6] came a fat woman with a smoky little

Statue of Charles IV on Křížovnické náměstí (1865)

lamp to see what had happened in the street. The piano playing stopped and a man now opened the half-open door completely. He spat grandly on a step and, while he was tickling the woman between her breasts, said that whatever had happened was not important anyway. At that they turned around and the door was shut once more.

When I tried to get up, I fell again. "It's black ice", I said and was conscious of a pain in my knee. But it still made me glad that the people from the tavern had not been able to see me, and therefore it seemed to me the most comfortable to remain lying here until dawn. ...

My acquaintance had his hands in his pockets and looked out along the empty bridge, then to the Kreuzherrenkirche [St. Francis Seraphin church], and then up to the sky, which was clear. As he had not been listening to me, he then said anxiously, "So why aren't you speaking, my friend? Don't you feel well? So why don't you get up? It's cold here, you will catch a chill, and anyway, we wanted to go up to Laurenziberg!"

Church of the Holy Saviour; right, in the shadow, Karlova street

"Of course", I said. "Forgive me." And I got up alone but in intense pain. I was swaying and had to look intently at the statue of Charles IV to be sure of my position. But the moonlight was clumsy and set Charles IV into motion too. I was astonished at this and my feet became much stronger out of the fear that Charles IV might fall over if I did not keep my composure. Later, my efforts seemed to me pointless since Charles IV fell down anyway, just as it occurred to me that I was loved by a girl in a beautiful white dress.

Franz Kafka, *Description of a Struggle*

Through the gate at the end of the lane one steps out onto Kreuzherrenplatz [Kří-žovnické náměstí]. To the right is the Clementinum with the Church of the Holly Savior. In front of the visitor is the St. Francis Seraphin Church; at the embankment, the Charles Monument. This monument was erected in 1848 to commemorate the 500-year jubilee of the founding of the university by Charles

St. Francis Seraphin church

IV. The 3.79-m-high figure of the Emperor in coronation robes rises from a pedestal holding the Foundation Charter in his right hand. The Faculties are mounted in four niches of the footstone: Theology at the front, Jurisprudence on the right, Medicine on the left and Philosophy at the back. On the corners are four friends of the Emperor, the ones at the front being: Ernst von Pardubitz and Johann Očko von Wlaschim, the first and second Archbishops of Prague; at the back: Benesch von Kolowrat, Charles' rescuer on the bridge to Pisa, and Mathias von Arras, the first architect of St. Vitus Cathedral at Hradčany. The plan for the beautiful monument was delivered by E. Hähnel in Dresden, it was cast by Burgschmiet in Nürnberg.

Griebens Reiseführer Prag, 1911

CHARLES BRIDGE
(Karlův most)

Then at once I knew all of the many stars by name, even though I had never learnt them. Yes, they were curious names, difficult to remember, but I knew them all and quite exactly. I raised my index finger and called them out individually. But I did not get very far with the naming of the stars, for I had to swim on if I did not want to sink. But so that no one could tell me later that just about anyone could swim across these cobblestones and it would not even be worth recounting, I raised myself swiftly up over the railing and, while swimming, circled each holy statue that I came across. At the fifth one, just as I was hoisting myself with deliberate strokes over the cobblestones, my acquaintance grabbed hold of my hand. I stood on the cobblestones and felt a pain in my knee. I had forgotten the names of the stars ...

Charles Bridge: View of Malá Strana bridge towers (around 1920)

My acquaintance pressed himself ever closer to me with his talk, and the moment I started to understand his words a white glimmer hopped delicately along the bridge railing, swept through the bridge tower and nipped into a dark lane. "I've always loved", said my acquaintance, pointing to the statue of Saint Ludmilla, "the hands of this angel on the left. Her tenderness is limitless and her outspread fingers tremble. But from this evening on I am indifferent to these hands, I can tell you, for I have kissed hands!" Thereupon he embraced me, kissed my clothes and thrust his head against my body.

Franz Kafka, *Description of a Struggle*

Here starts the oldest of Prague's bridges and the one most worth seeing: the famous Charles Bridge [Karlův most], which spans the 332-m-wide river. With its 16 arches, it is 505 m long and connects the Old Town with Malá Strana. The bridge does not run straight, but is crooked on each shore.

In 1153–1167 Judith, wife of Vladislav I, had a stone bridge built on the place where the previous wooden bridge

The statue of St. Ludmilla on Charles Bridge

had been destroyed by floods in 1118; once again it was destroyed in 1342 by an ice drift. A remnant of this is the quay wall facing the Křižovnické monastery with the chiselled head, an old benchmark. In 1357 Emperor Charles IV laid the foundation for the new construction with Peter Parler of Gmünd as the architect; the bridge was not completed until 1503. The strength of the stone Charles Bridge, which staunchly survived military attacks as well as countless floods, circulated in the vernacular of many legends. Naturally, the population was seized with great horror when in the flood of September 4,1890, two arches – the sixth and the seventh – plunged into the rising Moldau (Vltava) flood tide, which also cost two people their lives. After two years' work the bridge once again passed into general use.

Griebens Reiseführer Prag, 1911

There is within everyone a devil which gnaws the nights to destruction, and that is neither good nor bad, rather, it is life: if you did not have it, you could not live. So what you curse in yourself is your life. This devil is the material (and a fundamentally wonderful one) which you have been given and which you must now make use of. If you worked on the land, then it was not an excuse, to my knowledge; rather, you have driven your devil there, just as one day one drives livestock which has until now only nourished itself in the small streets of Teplice, onto better pastures. On the Charles Bridge in Prague, there is a relief under the statue of a saint, which tells your story. The saint is ploughing a field there and has harnessed a devil to the plough. Of course, the devil is still furious (hence the transitional stage; as long as the devil is not satisfied the victory is not complete), he bares his teeth, looks back at his master with a crooked, nasty expression and convulsively retracts his tail; nevertheless, he is submitted to the yoke. Now you, Minze, are no saint, of course, and should not even be one, and it is not at all necessary and would be sad and a pity if all your devils were to pull the plough, but for a great many of them it would be good, and it would have been a great, good deed that you had done thereby. I do not say this because it seems so only to me – you yourself are striving for this in your innermost.

Franz Kafka to Minze Eisner (1920)

In this citation, Kafka refers to a relief on the pedestal of the group statue "St. Vincentius Ferrerius and St. Procopius" (by Johann Brokoff), which stands on Charles Bridge. From Malá strana, it is the sixth statue on the right side of the bridge. St. Procopius, immigrant and founder of the venerable Szava Monastery, is a very popular saint in Bohemia. As a hermit, he is said to have tamed and subdued the Devil, who had wanted to lead him into temptation. Today, he lives on in the name of a small valley near Prague, where he supposedly lived in a cave.

> With Ottla. She is fetched by her English teacher. Over the quay, stone bridge, small piece of Malá strana, new bridge, home. Exciting statues of saints on Charles Bridge. The odd evening light of summertime when the bridge is deserted at night.
>
> from Franz Kafka's diaries (19. 6. 1919)

The relief on a Charles Bridge statue cited by Kafka

People who walk across dark bridges
Past saints
With dim lanterns

Clouds which drift across grey skies
Past churches
With sombre towers

Someone who leans against the solid railing
And gazes into the evening water
Hands on old stones.

Franz Kafka to Oskar Pollak (1903)

On Laurenziberg
(Petřín)

"How is that now", said my acquaintance, who had left
the party with me and was quietly walking beside me on
a path up Laurenziberg [Petřín]. "Stand still a moment,
so that I can get it all clear. You know, there's something
I have to settle. That is so strenuous-this cold but radiant
night, and still that discontented wind which sometimes
even appears to change the position of the acacias."

The shadow of the Gardener's House was cast over
the slightly humped path and decorated with scanty
patches of snow. When I glimpsed the bench, which
stood beside the door, I pointed at it with my raised
hand, but because I was not brave and expected reproaches, I laid my left hand on my breast.

He sat down wearily, without consideration for his
beautiful clothes, and astonished me by pressing his el-
bows against his hips and laying his forehead onto the
tips of his fully bent fingers.

Franz Kafka, *Description of a Struggle*

You reach Laurenziberg from Újezd. The streetcar goes
that far; on the uphill side of the street a narrow little
lane (K lanové dráze), near the Újezd barracks between
houses numbers 5 and 13, leads to the entrance of the
park. You can either climb the serpentine paths through
the lovely park on foot or take the funicular. Late afternoon is the recommended time to visit.

A second entrance leads from Welsche Gasse
[Vlašská] between the walls of the Lobkowitz and Strahov
gardens up over 266 stone steps in twenty minutes. This
route is advantageously used for the return trip. From the
Kinský Garden, too, you can reach the parks through the
Hunger Wall halfway up Laurenziberg.

Laurenziberg, 322 m high, is the easternmost foothill of
the White Mountain [Bílá hora]. It plays a prominent role in
the legends of Bohemia, for the pagan inhabitants of the
country are supposed to have sacrificed their gods here, and
Libuše is supposed to have prophesied the future greatness of
Prague from here. In 1360, Charles IV surrounded the hill

with a high jagged wall, which even now protrudes over the beautiful green beech wood and runs over the back of the hill from Strahov Monastery all the way down to Újezd. It bears the name Bread or Hunger Wall [Hladová zeď] because the Emperor had it erected during a famine, thereby providing a means of income for many people. Now it is broken through at one point, thus connecting the parks of Petřín with the Kinský Garden. [Note: the above-mentioned "Hunger Wall" inspired Franz Kafka to write *The Great Wall of China*.]

In the uppermost part of the parks is the restaurant Nebozízek with its magnificent view. Behind it the path leads to the St. Lawrence Church at the top of the hill. Built in 1770 on the same place as a chapel that already existed in the eleventh century, it houses some lovely paintings.

At the highest point of Laurenziberg stands a 60-m-high observation tower constructed of iron and modelled on the Eiffel Tower (384 m above sea level, ca. 200 m above the Moldau), built in 1891. The tower consists of two storeys of which the first is fitted with a circular gallery at a height of 20 m. The second storey is 54 m high. Both are accessible by means of either a comfortable, double 299-step staircase or an elevator.

The view of Prague and environs from the tower is exceptionally beautiful. One can see all the way to the Erzgebirge [Krušné hory] and over the picturesque Mittelgebirge [Středohoří] to the Isergebirge [Jizerské hory] and the Riesengebirge [Krkonoše], on the opposite side all the way to the Bohemian Forest [Šumava]. At ground level the observation tower offers a comfortable café and pub.

Griebens Reiseführer Prag, 1911

THE GARDENER'S HOUSE ON PETŘÍN

A short distance from the Nebozízek restaurant, located near the middle station of the cable railway, stands a dilapidated building, the "Gardener's House", which formerly served as the residence of the park gardener, and in front of which Kafka placed a scene in *Description of a Struggle*:

The observation tower on Petřín (around 1895)

It was very cold and the sky was already turning a bit whitish. Here no abomination will help, no disloyalty or journey to a faraway land. "You will have to murder yourself", I said, and also smiled ...

My acquaintance then drew a knife from his pocket without much ado, opened it thoughtfully and proceeded playfully to plunge it into his left upper arm and did not remove it. The blood began to flow immediately. His round cheeks were pale. I pulled out the knife, cut up the sleeve of his winter coat and tail coat, tore open the sleeve. I then ran up and down a short stretch of the path to see if there was anyone who could help. All the branches were sharply visible and motionless. Then I sucked a little on the deep wound. I then remembered the Gardener's House. I ran up the steps that led to the raised lawn on the left side of the house, I hastily investigated the windows and doors, I rang the bell, furious and stamping my feet, even though I had seen immediately that the house was unoccupied. Then I checked the

The dilapidated Gardener's House on Petřín

wound, which bled in a thin stream. I wet his scarf in the
snow and clumsily tied his arm.

Franz Kafka, Description of a Struggle

The student Kafka, in need of rest due to the strain of study,
spent his summer vacation of August 1905 in a sanatorium in
the Silesian village of Zuckmantel. An affair with an older
woman ("A woman, I inexperienced") provided Franz with
the needed change and his first deep romantic relationship.
He wrote to his friend Max Brod:

> Dear B.,
> Of course I would have written to you if I had stayed in
> Prague. I am, however, careless, already my fourth week
> in a sanatorium in Silesia, where I am very much among
> people and women and have become quite lively.
> Franz K.

Franz Kafka to Max Brod (1905)

Before Kafka returned to Prague to devote himself to his up-
coming examination, he spent a few weeks visiting relatives in
the southern Bohemian city of Strakonice. The ensuing weeks
allowed little time for student amusements. Preparations for
the examination became "the center of the sad world".

On November 7, he passed the second oral part of his docto-
ral examination (civic, commercial and bill-of-exchange law).

Malá Strana rooftops with the Prague Castle

In reality, the intellectual Prague of that Czech-German-Austrian-Jewish synthesis which made the city metropolitan and inspired it over centuries ended with Kafka.

Johannes Urzidil, *There Goes Kafka*

1906
DOCTORATE

After Kafka just barely passed his third oral examination (general and Austrian public law, international law and political economics), as well as, unanimously, oral examination I (Roman, canonical and German law), nothing stood in the way of his graduating.

Franz Kafka received his Doctor of Law degree on June 18, 1906, at a ceremony held in the assembly hall of the venerable Carolinum of the Karl-Ferdinand University in Prague (final grade: satisfactory). During the exam period Kafka had already, as of April 1, 1906, been working as an apprentice attorney in the legal office of Dr. Richard Löwy at Old Town Square 16.

After staying with his uncle Dr. Siegfried Löwy in Triesch, Kafka finally started his year in court, obligatory for the civil service, first in the Federal Civil Court on Ovocný trh 14, then in the Federal Criminal Court on Karlovo náměstí (near the New Town Hall, Novoměstská radnice). At this time, he wrote the novel fragment *Wedding Preparations in the Country.*

District courthouse on Karlsplatz (Karlovo náměstí)

THE COURTHOUSE AT OBSTMARKT
Ovocný trh 14/Celetná 36, Praha 1

The present-day courthouse was built on the foundations of a residential building, which in 1409 came into
the possession of King Wenceslas IV, who incorporated
it into the complex of the royal court. It served as the
royal mint from the time of the Hussite wars to 1783;
from 1784 it served as the Prague military headquarters.
Its present function stems from the middle of the eight-
eenth century. The building was erected by the Master
Minter Franz Josef Pachta of Rájov, according to the
plans of J.J. Wirch. The portal figures by Ignaz Franz
Platzer, which portray miners and soldiers as well as support the balcony, point to the previous functions of the
building. Since 1850, it has been a courthouse; for this
purpose an extension (1857–1858) by J. Malíček was
built in the direction of Obstmarkt, in Neo-Baroque
style.

Courthouse at Obstmarkt (Ovocný trh)

On June 12, 1848, at the outbreak of the Pentecost Revolution in Prague, the first battles with the troops of General Windischgrätz, the commanding officer of Prague, took place in front of this building. Due to a misdirected shot fired from the hotel across the street (House At the Golden Angel), Princess Marie Eleonore Windischgrätz, née Princess Schwarzenberg, sister of Prime Minister Felix Schwarzenberg, and of the Salzburger, later Prague, Cardinal Friedrich Schwarzenberg, was shot while standing at the window of the drawing room.

The courthouse was the scene of the professional activity of many lawyers, among them Franz Kafka and Max Brod. The seemingly endless passages of this labyrinth of courtrooms, offices and waiting rooms made their contribution to the physical landscape of Franz Kafka's novel *The Trial.*

Hugo Rokyta, *Die Böhmischen Länder: Prag*

Hermann Kafka's shop had already, for reasons of space, been moved to Celetná 12, where it would remain until September 1907. The rapid series of the company's location changes testified to the ascendance of the Kafka enterprise.

Balcony of the building housing Hermann Kafka's business, Celetná 12

Emperor Franz Joseph (from a 1915 oil painting by Robert Schiffer)

1907
Employment
at the Assicurazioni Generali

Kafka spent the summer of 1907 again at his uncle's in Triesch. There he met Hedwig Weiler, a Moravian of Jewish descent, and fell in love. Soon, however, Kafka began to neglect the girl, who was studying philosophy in Vienna, as he increasingly devoted his energies to his literary pursuits. He nevertheless dreamt of studying at the Vienna Export Academy in order to be close to Hedwig.

In October 1907 Franz Kafka took his first job, in the narrower sense of the term, at the insurance company Assicurazioni Generali on Wenceslas Square. The building was erected in 1900 in Prague Baroque style and can still be visited today.

> Now at the office. I am with Assicurazioni Generali and I hope at least one day to be able to sit in the armchairs of very distant lands, see sugarcane fields or Mohammedan cemeteries from the office windows; the insurance business itself interests me very much but my present work is sad. But it is still occasionally pleasant to put down the pen and imagine perhaps placing your hands one atop the other, clasping them with one hand and knowing that one would never let go of them, even if one's hand were screwed out of its wrist.
>
> Franz Kafka to Hedwig Weiler (1907)

After only a few months Kafka started looking for a more comfortable job. The working hours at the Generali were too long for him, and the idea of soon serving the interesting

Building of the Assicurazioni Generali on Wenceslas Square

insurance business in distant countries, with a view of "Mohammedan cemeteries" and the like, turned out to be nothing but romantic illusion which, if at all, could become reality only after many years had passed. Franz Kafka served as a temporary employee daily from 8:00 a.m. until, not infrequently, 8:30 p.m., with only seven days of vacation per year and a salary of 80 crowns per month. Those were decidedly harsh working conditions for a young man with a body weight of 61 kg and a height of 182 cm (according to the medical examination at the time, taken when starting a new job).

Wenceslas Square (around 1895)

He slaved away at the private insurance company called Assicurazoni Generali that had its splendid seat on the corner of Wenceslas Square and Heinrichsgasse (Jindřišská). He slaved away even though as literary and equally educated as his sarcastic boss, Director Eisner (a close relative of Paul Eisner, later to become a well-known translator into Czech, and author), treated him very kindly.

Max Brod, About Franz Kafka

Curriculum Vitae
I was born in Prague on July 3, 1883, attended the Old Town Elementary School until fourth grade, then entered the Old Town German State Secondary School; at eighteen years of age I began my studies at the German Karl-Ferdinand University in Prague. After passing my final state exam, I joined the legal office of Dr. Richard Löwy in Old Town Square as an articled clerk on April 1, 1906. In June I took the final comprehensive exams in history and in the same month was conferred the Doctor of Law degree.

I joined the chambers just as I had agreed with Dr. Löwy from the beginning, only to make the most of my time, for right from the beginning I did not have the intention of staying at the legal office. On October 1, 1906, I entered legal practice and remained there until October 1, 1907.

Dr. Franz Kafka (1907)

At this time, the family shop was moved into the Kinský Palace in Old Town Square. This change of address provided visible evidence of the prosperity of the Kafka business.

Thus it is not surprising that Kafka was commended in a report by the Generali Insurance company: "He comes from a respected family."

In June of the same year the family had moved from the medieval house "At the Three Kings" into the stylish Pařížská street. The new building "At the Ship", Pařížská 36, was one of the most recently built rental mansions for which the ancient Prague Ghetto had been sacrificed. The building "At the Ship" is no longer extant; it was destroyed in 1945.

Franz Kafka at 27 years of age

An entry in Kafka's diary conveys an impression of his room in the upper storey (the third, according to official classification) of this fashionable building (which naturally had a lift):

On the sofa toward evening in the darkness of my room. Why does it take longer to recognise a colour but after turning the decisive curve of comprehension we quickly become more convinced about the colour. If the light from the anteroom and that from the kitchen strike the glass door at the same time, greenish or, better, not to devalue the certain impression, green light flows all the way down the panes. If the light in the anteroom is turned off and the kitchen light remains on, the pane nearest the kitchen turns deep blue, the other whitish blue, so whitish that the entire drawing on the matte glass (stylised poppyheads, tendrils, diverse rectangles and leaves) dissolves.

The lights and shadows thrown onto the walls and ceiling by the electric lights of the streets and bridge below are in disarray and in part ruined covering each other and hard to scrutinise...

There was just no domestic consideration given at the installation of the electric lights down there and at the arrangement of this room as to how my room would look from the sofa at this hour without its own lighting. – The glow thrown upon the ceiling by the tram passing below runs whitish, mysterious and mechanically faltering along the one wall and the ceiling, broken at the seam. – The globe stands in the first fresh full reflection of the streetlight on the from above greenish pure over-illuminated linen-basket, has a highlight on its curvature, as if the glow is too strong for it, although the light passes over its smoothness and leaves it looking rather brownish, leather-apple-like. – The light from the anteroom produces a broad glow on the wall above the bed that is limited to a curved line from the head of the bed, depresses the sight of the bed, diffuses the dark bedposts, raises the ceiling above the bed.

from Franz Kafka's diaries (4. 10. 1911)

In this room Franz Kafka would write his great story *The Judgement* during the now legendary night of September 22–23, 1912. *The Metamorphosis* and *Lost Without a Trace* also originated in this room.

Franz Kafka could look out of his bedroom window onto the newly built Čech Bridge, built in 1908.

> The sight of the stairs grips me so today. From already early on and many times since, I have enjoyed the sight from my window of the triangular section of the stone railing of that staircase which leads from the right of Čech Bridge [Čechův most] down to the quay platform. Very slanted, as though it were giving only a brief, faint suggestion. And there, on the other side of the river, I now see a ladder on the embankment which leads to the water. It has always been there but is revealed only in autumn and winter with the removal of the swimming school, which is otherwise in front of it, and is lying over there in the dark grass under the brown trees in the play of perspectives.
>
> from Franz Kafka's diaries (29. 9. 1911)

Kafka had already mentioned the construction of this bridge in a letter to Hedwig Weiler:

> I spent last week truly in the street in which I live and which I call 'Run-up Street for Suicides' because this street broadly leads to the river, a bridge is being built there, and the Belvedere on the other bank, these are hills and gardens, will be tunnelled under so that people can walk along the street across the bridge below the Belvedere. For now, this is only amusement because it will always be more pleasant to walk across the bridge up to the Belvedere than through the river to Heaven.
>
> Franz Kafka to Hedwig Weiler (1908)

The topographic relationship to Čech Bridge is also clearly described in the concluding sequence of "The Judgement":

> He sprang through the door, it drove him across the street down to the river. Now he grasped the railing like a hungry man his food. He swung himself over like the excellent gymnast who had been his parents' pride in his youth. He still held on with weakening hands, spotted between the bars of the railing a bus which would easily drown out his fall, called out quietly: "Dear parents, I have always loved you", and let himself fall.
> At that moment an almost endless stream of traffic crossed the bridge.
>
> Franz Kafka, *The Judgement*

Čech Bridge (Čechův most), with the newly built apartment building "At the Ship" seen behind the bridge's right-hand support column (around 1807)

1908 – 1911

THE FIRST YEARS AT THE "ARBEITER-UNFALL-VERSICHERUNGSANSTALT"
(WORKER'S ACCIDENT INSURANCE COMPANY FOR THE KINGDOM OF BOHEMIA)

Na Poříčí 7, Praha 1

As of July 30, 1908, the year in which Kafka's short prose pieces *Meditation* first appeared in the magazine *Hyperion*, he was employed as a temporary officer for the Worker's Accident Insurance Company, by far the largest institution of its kind in the entire Hapsburg Monarchy, and he was to remain an employee until his early retirement in 1920. The institution of a worker's insurance organization was established in the old Austria in the year 1889.

The father of Kafka's schoolmate Ewald Felix Přibram (Dr. Otto Přibram) had been president of the company since 1895. Thanks to this connection, Kafka was able to obtain this otherwise hard-to-get position in the half-state-owned organisation.

The building which housed the institution was completed in 1896 and serves a different purpose today; yet with a bit of imagination one can still picture Kafka's working world very well. At the beginning, Kafka's office was situated in the top storey; later, it was in the first, the same storey as the office of the president, Dr. Otto Přibram.

Building that once housed the Worker's Accident Insurance Company

105

This position in this institute suited Kafka far better than his occupation at the Generali. His workday was only from 8:00 a.m. to 2:00 p.m., hardly more than part-time, and he did not earn too badly.

Franz Kafka developed into a considerably skilled insurance expert. In the beginning he had to classify the businesses he was in charge of according to their degree of danger, and also to visit and inspect them. Kafka's responsibilities included representing his insurance company in matters before the court, drawing up statistics, keeping independent correspondence, processing workers' accident insurance claims and much more.

> In my four chief districts – with the exception of the rest of my work – the people fall as if drunk from the scaffolding and into the machines, all the beams tip over, the whole riverbank loosens, all the ladders slip out from under; whatever is raised up plunges to the ground, whatever is taken down one stumbles over. And one gets a headache from all these young girls in the porcelain factories who are forever throwing themselves down the stairs with mountains of dishes.
>
> Franz Kafka to Max Brod (1909)

The fact that Kafka did not lose his post with the founding of Czechoslovakia in 1918 is of some interest. His German-speaking superiors, Eugen Pfohl and Robert Marschner, were certainly dismissed and replaced by Czechs. However, Kafka himself was able to hold on, on the one hand because he was well protected by patronage, and on the other hand because of the fact that he had kept his distance from all German patriotic actions.

During his twelve-year professional career with this insurance company Kafka rose from being a temporary clerk to chief secretary (1910, clerk; 1913, vice-secretary; 1920, secretary). Kafka was highly regarded by his colleagues and superiors and was often praised by them.

> When we had both attained the hoped-for occupation "with simple frequency" (that is to say, without after-

noon shift) it so happened that the way home from our offices was the same. So every day at 2:00 p.m. I waited for Franz at the Pulverturm [Powder Tower] – how well and in what detail I studied the old elaborate two-headed imperial eagle on the gable of the Financial Office, at the corner of Hibernergasse [Hybernská], for Franz came later than I, he still had official things to do or lost himself in conversations with colleagues – with a growling stomach I patrolled up and down, but the anger was quickly forgotten when the tall, slender form of my friend appeared, usually wearing an embarrassed smile which was meant to pretend rather than really express great dismay, indeed horror, at his long delay.

With this he would press his hand to his heart. This gesture meant, "I am innocent". Moreover, he arrived trotting at a fast pace, so that you really could not say anything too severe to him. There was always an infinite amount to discuss on our common path through Zeltnergasse Also we never found the last word in front of Franz's door for a long time. And then in the afternoon or evening we were together again.

Max Brod, *About Franz Kafka*

The Powder Tower (1911); beside it, the Municipal House (Obecní dům)

Kafka kept a diary since his student days. His notes, written down since 1909 and preserved to this day, are – like Kafka's letters – a major part of his production and a key to his life and work. They often refer to Prague sites with which he was familiar:

> Yesterday evening on Schützeninsel [Střelecký ostrov], didn't find my colleagues and left immediately. I created some stir with my frock coat and the crushed soft hat in my hands, because it was cold outside but here it was hot from the breaths of the beer-drinkers, smokers and horns of the military band. This band was not too high up, and it couldn't be because the hall is rather low and it filled one end of the hall all the way to the side-walls. This crowd of musicians was shoved into this end of the hall as if especially fitted. This impression of being crammed was lost somewhat in the hall, as most of the seats near the band were vacant and the hall was only filled in the middle.
>
> from Franz Kafka's diaries (13. 10. 1911)

Contemporary military orchestra (1864)

THE HOUSE OF THE FORMER GERMAN COMMERCIAL COLLEGE
Masná 8, Praha 1

Between February and May 1908 Kafka attended a course at this institution, at which the writer Gustav Meyrink passed his school-leaving examination and the poet and translator Rudolf Fuchs also attended a course.

> The institute, owned by the Chamber of Commerce and highly regarded in Prague business circles, was attended not only by Germans but also by many Czechs. The Business Academy was founded in 1856 as the first establishment of higher education for business on the territory of the imperial and royal monarchy. Franz Kafka, who completed a course in worker's insurance here in 1908, is undoubtedly the most famous student of the institute.
>
> Hugo Rokyta, *Die Böhmischen Länder: Prag*

Former German Commercial Academy

French military aeroplane „Astra" (around 1912)

Granted an exceptional eight-day holiday in September 1909, Kafka travelled with Max and Otto Brod to Riva on Lake Garda and from there visited an aeronautic exhibition and flying demonstration in Brescia. The text "The Aeroplanes from Brescia", written during the journey, can be re-

Aeroplane over Chuchle

garded as one of the first literary descriptions of modern aeroplanes in German literature. On September 29 of the same year a shortened version of the text appeared in the Prague German-language newspaper *Bohemia*.

After his return to Prague, Kafka began work on the second version of *Description of a Struggle*. A few months later, in March 1910, *Bohemia* published extracts from the work.

At this time Kafka came into contact with Bar-Kochba, the Association of Jewish Students, and with it the Zionist movement, which in those years represented the major alternative to the path of assimilation of his father's generation. Kafka also wanted to free himself of his father's half-hearted religious conviction:

> It was really, as far as I could tell, a mere trifle, a joke, not even a joke. You went to the temple four days a year, where you were, to say the least, closer at least to the indifferent than to those who took it seriously, patiently went through the prayers as a formality, sometimes amazed me by being able to show me in the prayer book the passage that was just

The Old-New Synagogue in Prague's Jewish ghetto (around 1865)

being recited, and other than that, so long as I was (and this was the main thing) present in the synagogue I was allowed to hang around wherever I wanted. So I yawned and dozed away the many hours there (I don't think I was ever so bored again until dancing lessons) and tried as best I could to enjoy the few small diversions there were, for instance, when the Ark of the Covenant was opened, which always reminded me of the shooting galleries where a cupboard door would open whenever you hit a bull's eye, only there something interesting always came out, and here it was always the same old dolls without heads. Incidentally, I was also very frightened there, not only, of course, because of all the people one came into contact with, but also because you once mentioned in passing that I too might be called to the Torah. That was something I dreaded for years. But other than that I was not fundamentally disturbed in my boredom, perhaps by the bar-mitzvah, but that only required some ridiculous rote learning, in other words, it led only to a ridiculous passing of an exam, and then, what concerns you, by small, not very significant incidents, like when you were called to the Torah and did well in what felt to me purely a social event, or when you remained in the temple for the prayers for the dead and I would be sent away,

Interior of the Old-New Synagogue (1870)

Tombstone in the Old Jewish Cemetery in Prague (1865)

which, for a long time – apparently because of having been sent away, and the lack of any deeper interest – gave rise in me to a feeling I was hardly aware of, that something indecent was going on. That's how it was in the synagogue; at home it was, if possible, even shabbier and limited to the first Seder, which developed increasingly into a farce with fits of laughter, admittedly under the influence of the maturing children. (Why did you have to give way to this influence? Because you brought it about.) This, then, was the religious material that was handed down to me, added to this was at most the outstretched hand pointing to 'the sons of the millionaire Fuchs', who on the high holy days came to the synagogue with their father. I did not understand how to do anything better with this material than get rid of it as quickly as possible; precisely this ridding myself of it seemed to me the most pious act.

Franz Kafka, Letter to his father

In 1910, eastern European Jewish actors performed in Prague. Kafka, taken by Max Brod on May 4 to a performance, observed with fascination eastern Jewish folklore and its characteristic religiousness and peculiarities. When, in the fall of 1911, Jizchak Löwy, who came from the Jewish theatre in Warsaw, gave his first performance at the Café Savoy on Ziegenplatz, which Kafka attended with Brod, it served as the prelude to an enduring and intense preoccupation with eastern Judaism. Kafka saw in it not only an unspent, fresh and traditional spirituality, but also the beginnings of his own, personal Judaism.

Kafka attended the 20 performances of this theatre troupe from Galicia. He committed himself to the "Lembergers" by reporting on them, through Max Brod, among others, in the *Prager Tagblatt* and in the Jewish weekly *Selbstwehr*, or by trying to line up guest appearances for them in the Bohemian provinces.

Building which once housed the Café Savoy; today a modest restaurant is housed in the ground floor

Vegetable market (around 1880)

This fascination is captured in his diary entries of the subsequent period, as is the disgust of his father, who had no use for these "ham actors":

> Löwy – my father about him: whoever lies down with dogs gets up with fleas. I could not help myself and said something inappropriate. Thereupon my father answered particularly calmly (albeit after a long pause, which was filled in another way): "You know that I must not get upset and I have to take it easy. So come on and do not start with such things. I have had enough excitement already, absolutely enough. Now leave me alone with such talk." I say, "I am making an effort to restrain myself", and feel from Father, as I always do in such extreme moments, the presence of a wisdom only a breath of which I can grasp.
>
> from Franz Kafka's diaries (2. 11. 1911)

In October of the same year Kafka travelled to Paris with Max and Otto Brod, and then in December to Berlin.

THE PUBLIC SWIMMING SCHOOL
AT ČECH BRIDGE
(Občanská plovárna)

When it was warm, Kafka liked to go to the public baths on Žofín and often also swam at the Public Swimming School on the Malostranská bank of the Vltava. Kafka owned his own boat there, called, in the language of the time, *Seelentränker* (Soulsoaker), in which he often and happily went rowing on the Vltava. Parts of the shiny white facility, founded in 1840, can still be seen today, although it is no longer possible to swim there. However, whoever wishes to experience the atmosphere of a public baths from that era can in summer go to the "Yellow Baths" (Žluté lázně) in Podoli in the south of Prague and there swim in the cool Vltava.

> The period which has now passed and in which I have not written a word has been important for me because while at the swimming schools in Prague, Königssaal [Zbraslav] and Czernoschitz [Černošice], I have stopped feeling ashamed of my body. How late in life I am making up for my upbringing, now at the age of 28; in a race

Former Public Swimming School near the Čech Bridge

Scene from the Public Swimming School (turn of the century)

this would be considered a late start. And the harm in such a misfortune perhaps does not consist in not winning; the latter is, of course, still only the visible, certain, healthy core of the ever blurring and never-ending ill fortune which drives me, who is supposed to run around the edge of the circle, into the inner part of the circle.

from Franz Kafka's diaries (15. 8. 1911)

A few years ago I was often in my Soulsoaker on the Vltava, I rowed up and then, all stretched out, floated down with the current, passing beneath the bridges. Because I was so thin, this might have looked very funny from the bridge. One civil servant who once saw me like that from the bridge summed up his impressions – after he had sufficiently emphasized the comical aspect – as follows: It looked like the Last Judgement. It was like that moment when the coffin lids have been removed but the dead still lay there motionless.

Franz Kafka to Milena Jesenská (1920)

We spent countless splendid hours on the planks of the Prague swimming facilities, in boats on the Vltava, doing climbing tricks on the weir, a good many reflections of which can be found in my novel *Stefan Rott*. I admired Franz's swimming and rowing abilities, he could steer a so-called Soulsoaker particularly skillfully. He was always defter and bolder than I and had a certain way of leaving you in breakneck situations, and with an almost cruel smile (which meant something like: "Save yourself"), to your fate. How I loved this smile which contained so much confidence and encouragement! Franz was inexhaustible, so it seemed to me, in inventing new variations of sports. His personality expressed itself even in this; even this he did (as everything else) with complete dedication.

Max Brod, *About Franz Kafka*

... once in autumn, I think, or already in spring, I don't know, I went boating with Ottla and the little Růženka – who had prophesied in the Schönborn Palace that my end was near. In front of the Rudolfinum we met Haas with a woman whom I didn't look at at all, that was Jarmila. Haas told her my name and Jarmila remarked that she had spoken to my sister at the Public Swimming School many years ago; she had kept her in mind as a Jewish curiosity, since the Swimming School was very Christian at the time. We lived opposite it in those days and Ottla showed her our flat.

Franz Kafka to Milena Jesenská (1920)

In the literary and intellectual life of the Prague of that time, just as in Vienna or Berlin, cafés played a major role as cultural centres and meeting-places, whether they were named Arco or Continental, Louvre or Radetzky. Here one could read the latest newspapers, hear the latest gossip, hold discussions with like-minded acquaintances or just "be among the people". Here one regularly met members of diverse literary, philosophic or friendship circles, here was always place to compose a poem or write a review for one of the Prague papers. And if one didn't have enough money to buy wood or coal, here one had the chance to survive the days of bitter cold. And, of course, one could always have a cup of coffee or a little something to eat.

Kafka also enjoyed going to cafés:

> Dear Mr. Baum, I am writing this at 12 o'clock in the Continental, the first quiet place on this Saturday ...
>
> Franz Kafka to Oskar Baum (1907)

The interior of the café in the Municipal House (1912)

My dear Max – How about coming immediately to the Arco for just a little while, not for long, God forbid, only as a favour to me, you know, the Př. is here. Please Madam, please Mr. Brod, be so kind as to let Max come here. Franz K.

Franz Kafka to Max Brod (probably 1909)

Alternating feelings amidst the young people in Café Arco.

from Franz Kafka's diaries (25. 2. 1912)

Later, toward the end of World War I, Kafka told his blind friend, Oskar Baum, a story that suggests why Kafka, who on the one hand enjoyed being alone and, on the other hand, feared isolation, might have felt well in cafés:

A man wants to see about holding a party with people who come together without being invited. People see and observe and speak to one another, without knowing one another. It is a banquet that any of them, according to his tastes, can arrange to suit himself without being a burden on anyone else. One can appear and disappear again whenever one wants, has no obligation to a host and is nevertheless, without hypocrisy, always welcome. When the man actually succeeds in realising this droll idea, the reader recognises that also this attempt to relieve loneliness only – produced the inventor of the first café.

Franz Kafka to Oskar Baum (1918)

In January and February 1911, Franz Kafka travelled on business to Friedland (Frýdlant) and Reichenberg (Liberec). In the summer he went to Zürich, Lugano, Milano and Paris. This was followed by a week-long stay, in late summer, in the naturopathic sanatorium at Erlenbach near Zürich.

Kafka cultivated contacts with many important authors, not only of the Prague circle. He associated with the families Brod, Baum, Kisch and Werfel. Franz Werfel, whose literary circle (Willy Haas, Paul Kornfeld, Franz Janowitz, Rudolf

Fuchs, Otto Pick, Ernst Polak, among others) met in the Café
Arco, had been – unlike Kafka – an important and interna-
tionally renowned author since before World War I. The so-
phisticated and energetic Werfel, who was seven years younger
than Kafka, was increasingly accepted and even liked by the
shy and, at the beginning of their acquaintance, reserved
Kafka. However, a touch of jealousy must have played a constant role in their relationship.

> Max came yesterday from Berlin. However, in the
> *Berliner Tagblatt* he was called selfless by a Fackelmensch
> because he had read from the works of the "far more im-
> portant Werfel". Max had to cross out this sentence be-
> fore he brought the review to the *Prager Tagblatt*. I hate
> W. not because I envy him, but I also envy him. He is
> healthy, young and rich, I'm different in everything. In
> addition, he wrote very well, with a sense of music, early
> and easily, he has the happiest life behind him and before
> him, I work with weights that I cannot get rid of and I
> am totally separated from music.
>
> from Franz Kafka's diaries (18. 12. 1911)

Men of such significance as Kurt Tucholsky, Robert Musil or
Alfred Kubin were included among his acquaintances. Kurt
Tucholsky and the draughstman Kurt Szafranski visited him
and Max Brod in September 1911. Kafka himself, however,
was still a literary unknown.

Kafka's brother-in-law, Karl Hermann, founded the Prague
Hermann & Co. Asbestos Works after his marriage to Elli
Kafka. The designation "Co." referred to none other than
Franz Kafka, who, with his own money and his father's, became financially involved in this factory. Kafka's father would
not have minded seeing Franz in the role of an industrialist,
and finally began to criticise his son when he noticed that his
commitment to the factory was only half-hearted.

> The torment the factory brings me. Why did I not
> protest when I was obligated to work afternoons there.

Now, nobody is violently forcing me, but Father with reproaches, Karl with silence and my conscience. I know nothing about the factory and stood around uselessly and as if beaten during this morning's official inspection. I denied myself this opportunity to become acquainted with all of the factory's details.

from Franz Kafka's diaries (28. 12. 1911)

The factory, which employed 25 workers, was located in the workers' quarter of Žižkov (Bořivojova 27). For Kafka – who was unable to work up the slightest interest in the enterprise and also did not have the time to work there – the factory re-

In the courtyard of the former Hermann & Co. Asbestos Works

Workers (around 1890)

presented a considerable burden. This was especially true from the time the brother-in-law had to report to the military and he had often to look after the factory, which was shut down at the beginning of the war. As long as he had to go to the factory, he could not even begin to think about writing.

> Nothing written. Was in the factory and for 2 hours breathed gas in the engine room. The energy of the foreman and the stoker at the engine, which for some unknown reason does not want to start. Miserable factory.
>
> from Franz Kafka's diaries (10. 8. 1912)

The economic difficulties caused by the war finally resulted in the liquidation of the Hermann & Co. Asbestos Works in 1917.

Kafka had previously spoken about "this wretched sight of a factory". The following diary entry conveys just how much the "factory" affected Kafka's state of mind:

> Was reproached because of the factory the day before yesterday. Then spent an hour on the sofa thinking about jumping out the window.
>
> from Franz Kafka's diaries (8. 3. 1912)

My dear Max! ... My brother-in-law the industrialist left early today – which in my happy state of distraction I hardly noticed – on a business trip that will last 10 to 14 days. During this time, the factory is actually in the hands of the foreman alone, and no investor, and how much less so such a nervous one as my father, will have any doubt about the fraudulent business that is now going on at the factory. Incidentally, I believe the same, but not really from fear about the money as from ignorance and an uneasy conscience. Finally, even someone not involved, to the extent I can envisage him, should not doubt my father's right to be afraid, even if I must not forget that at bottom I do not at all understand why a foreman who is a citizen of the German empire, even in the absence of my brother-in-law, to whom he is infinitely superior in all technical and organisational matters, cannot run everything in the same manner as usual, because in the end we are all human beings and not thieves.

Franz Kafka to Max Brod (1912)

Yesterday at the factory. The girls – in their unbearably filthy and loose dresses, with their hair tousled as if they'd just awoken, with their expressions fixed by the ceaseless noise of the transmissions and the automatic but unpredictably faltering machines – are not human beings, one doesn't greet them, one doesn't apologise when bumping into them, if you call them for some small task, they carry it out and immediately return to their machines, one shows them where they should take hold, they stand there in their slips, are vulnerable to the slightest power and don't even possess enough calm understanding to acknowledge this power with glances and bows and to show themselves willing. Comes six o'clock, however, and they announce it to each other, they untie the kerchiefs from their necks and hair, dust themselves off with a brush that is passed around the hall and called for by the impatient, pull their skirts over their heads and clean their hands as best they can, and in the end they really are women, are able to smile despite their pallor and bad teeth, shake their stiff bodies, you cannot bump

View of the Prague industrial district Smíchov (1867)

into, look at or overlook them, you press yourself against the greasy boxes to make way for them, hold your hat in your hands when they say good evening and you don't know how to react when one of them holds your winter jacket so that you can put it on.

from Franz Kafka's diaries (8. 2. 1912)

Yesterday at the factory. Returned by tram, sat in a corner with legs outstretched, saw people outside, lit shoplamps, walls with viaducts passing through them, again and again backs and faces leading out of the main shopping street of the suburb, a country road with nothing more human than people going home, the piercing electric lights of the train station grounds burned into the darkness, the low, markedly tapered chimneys of a gasworks, a poster announcing the performance of a female singer de Treville which gropes its way along the walls up to a street near the cemeteries, from where it then returns again with me from the cold of the fields to the homely warmth of the city ... That's why I always arrive at the suburbs with mixed feelings of fear, of being abandoned, of pity, of curiosity, of pride, of joy of travel, of manliness, and return with contentment, seriousness, and tranquillity; especially from Žižkov.

from Franz Kafka's diaries (18. 11. 1911)

125

At home, however, Kafka expected anything but tranquillity. No one took into consideration his sensitivity to noise. Therefore, he wrote in his diary, with resignation:

> I want to write with a continual trembling on my forehead. I sit in my room in the headquarters of the noise from the entire apartment. I hear the slamming of every door, their noise only spares me the sound of the footsteps of those who walk through them, and I also hear the clapping shut of the oven doors in the kitchen. Father bursts through the door to my room dragging his dressing-gown behind him, the ashes are scraped from the oven in the adjoining room, Valli asks through the anteroom as if calling into uncertainty through a Paris street if Father's hat has been cleaned yet, a hissing that wants to be intimate with me raises the scream of an answering voice. The apartment door is unlatched and sounds like the noise made by a catarrhal throat, then opens wide with the brief singing of a woman's voice and shuts with a dull, manly jolt that sounds the most inconsiderate. Father is gone, now begins the more tender, more dispersed, more hopeless noise, led by the voices of the two canaries. I had already thought of it earlier, it occurs to me again because of the canaries, if I shouldn't open the door a bit, crawl like a snake into the next room and, thus on the floor, beg my sister and her little miss for quiet.
>
> from Franz Kafka's diaries (5. 11. 1911)

It is therefore no wonder that Kafka tried to find peace and quiet by taking long, solitary walks:

> Nice solitary walk to those amusing places in R. and S. across the Castle and Belvedere. In Nerudová a sign: Anna Křižová, Taylor, apprenticed in France with the duchess-widow Ahrenberg née Princess Ahrenberg. — I stood in the middle of the first Castle courtyard and watched the Castle guard on alert.
>
> from Franz Kafka's diaries (8. 12. 1911)

Absolute uselessness. Sunday. Particular insomnia during the night. Until 1/4 to 12 in bed while the sun shone. Walk. Lunch. Read newspaper, skimmed through old catalogues. Walked down Hibernerstraße [Hybernská], city park, Wenceslas Square, Ferdinandstraße [Ferdinandská], then walked toward Podoli. Strenuously prolonged to 2 hours.

from Franz Kafka's diaries (21. 11. 1911)

Kafka also often strolled through the city with friends, acquaintances and relatives:

Walk with Löwy to the Governor's Castle, which I called Zion Fortress. The tracery of the entrance gates and the colour of the sky went clearly together. – Another walk to Hetzinsel.

from Franz Kafka's diaries (8. 12. 1911)

Walk with Löwy down to the river. The one pillar of the arch, which rises up on the Elisabeth Bridge [Eliščin most] and is internally illuminated by an elec. lamp, as a dark mass between light streaming from the sides, looked like a factory chimney, and the dark wedge of shadow stretching to the sky above it was like rising smoke. The sharply restricted green light-surfaces at the side of the bridge.

from Franz Kafka's diaries (14. 12. 1911)

Then walk with Ottla, Miss Taussig, Mr. and Mrs. Baum and Pick, Elisabeth Bridge, the quay, Radetzky Café, Charles Bridge, Karlsgasse. I still had the prospect of a good mood, so that there was nothing really wrong with me.

from Franz Kafka's diaries (2. 3. 1912)

Among Kafka's favourite destinations for his excursions through Prague was the Chotek Parkgrounds located far from the city's bustle, directly adjoining the royal pleasure palace, the Belvedere, behind the Castle.

Brückengasse (Mostecká), with the St. Nicholas Church in the background

Today partially beautiful Sunday. In the Chotek grounds, read Dostojevsky's written defence. The Castle guard and at corps headquarters. The fountain at the Thun Palace. – Much self-satisfaction the whole day. And now utter failure at work.

from Franz Kafka's diaries (1. 11. 1914)

In the morning: in bed until 1/2 12. A jumble of thoughts that slowly forms and hardens in an incredible manner. Read in the morning (Gogol, essay on poetry)

evening walk in part with the enduring but untrustwor-
thy thoughts from morning. Sat in the Chotek grounds.
Most beautiful place in Prague. Birds sang, the Castle
with the gallery, the old trees hung with last year's fo-
liage, the half-darkness. Later Ottla came with D.

from Franz Kafka's diaries (14. 3. 1915)

Incapable of writing a single line. The well-being with
which I sat yesterday in the Chotek grounds and today
on Karlsplatz [Karlovo náměstí] with Strindberg's "On
the Open Sea". The well-being today in my room.
Hollow as a shell on the beach, ready to be crushed un-
derfoot.

from Franz Kafka's diaries (23. 3. 1915)

Nothing, dull slightly aching head. Afternoon Chotek
parkgrounds, read Strindberg, who nourishes me.

from Franz Kafka's diaries (5. 5. 1915)

The Chotek Parkgrounds with the Belvedere pleasure palace

1912 – 1913
ACQUAINTANCE
WITH FELICE BAUER

On February 18, 1912, Franz Kafka introduced a lecture evening held by the Jewish actor Jizchak Löwy, with whom he would remain in close contact for many years, in the main hall of the Jewish Town Hall. The main hall can still be seen today. On December 11, 1913, Kafka read for the second time in the Jewish Town Hall – this time in the setting of a charity event – from Kleist's *Michael Kohlhaas*.

THE JEWISH TOWN HALL
Maislová ulice 18, Praha 1

The Jewish Town Hall, built in the 1580s by Master Pankraz, stands in close proximity to the Old-New Synagogue. The construction was financed by the wealthy Mordechaj Maisl.

The Jewish Town Hall houses the seat of the council of the Jewish Religious Community, a ceremonial banquet hall and the offices of the Prague Jewish Community. The Jewish Museum, with its superb collection of ceremonial textiles

The clocks on the Jewish Town Hall

Anzeige im ›Börsenblatt‹ vom 18. November 1912

Advert for Kafka's first book in the *German Book Trade Gazette*
(November 1912)

(curtains from synagogues from all over Europe, Torah coverings etc.) is also located in the building.

After the Swedish siege in 1648, the Jews were granted the right to build a Town Hall tower as a reward for their military service. The Town Hall was reconstructed in1763 and provided with a rococo facade and a wooden tower. It is adorned with two clocks, one with Latin and the other with Hebraic numerals.

At the beginning of the year 1912 Kafka was working on his first draft and chapters of the work *Lost Without Trace.* (Max Brod later published it under the title *Amerika.*)

Throughout July, after three weeks at the Jungborn Naturopathic Sanatorium in the Harz Mountains, he was in Weimar with Max Brod. The next month, Kafka compiled the texts for his first book, *Meditation*, which was eventually published by the aspiring Rowohlt Publishing House in December of that year.

> Kafka's small meditations provided something as yet unfamiliar in German literature; I did not know of any precedent. Very quietly, joining some passages of Brod's, they surpass with often marvelous power Brod in the art of resolving some momentary sensation or atmosphere into their final elements, mostly to bind them to objects, and with the love that is unique to this circle of writers to place themselves in the interior of objects and people, as for example that salesman. There are pieces there, such as the "Late Walk", that take one's breath away, strange, eerie and utterly incomprehensible stories, such as "Unhappiness", which recall Kubin. They completely dissolve one's mood and are just as difficult to resist as the infinitely generous, perhaps ultimately somewhat sentimental love which arises from "Passenger". This love matters to Kafka's nature just as it does to Werfel's; only that Kafka's love is always very silent in itself, whereas Werfel places love everywhere before us in his poems, and no doubt is therefore much more popular.
> Hans Kohn

Towards the end of the year the story *The Metamorphosis* appeared.

In one of the first public readings in Prague – held by the Johann Gottfried Herder Association under the leadership of Willy Haas – Kafka read from *The Judgement* in the Mirror Room of the Hotel Erzherzog Stefan (today Hotel Evropa). In a diary entry dated September 23, 1912, Kafka described the origin of this story:

> I wrote this story, *The Judgement*, in one go, on the night of the 22nd to 23rd from 10:00 p.m. to 6:00 a.m. I could hardly pull my legs, which had got stiff from sitting, from under the desk. The terrible effort and joy as this story unfolded before me, as I progressed through slow waters. Many times throughout this night, I carried a great weight upon my back. How everything can be risked, just as for everyone a great fire is prepared for the strangest ideas in which they die and rise again. How it started turning blue at the window. A car driving past. Two men crossing the bridge. At 2:00 a.m. I looked at the clock for the last time. When the servant girl walked through the anteroom for the first time today, I was writing down the last sentence.
>
> The extinguishing of the lamp, and the light of day. The light stabbing chest pains. The passing sleepiness in the middle of the night. Tremblingly entering the room of my sisters. The public reading. Before, the stretching out of myself in front of the servant girl and saying: "I have been writing until now." The appearance of the untouched bed as though it had just been carried in. The complete conviction that I find my writing of novels at a shamefully low level. This is the only way to write, only in such a context with such a complete opening of the body and the soul. The morning in bed. The constantly clear eyes. Many feelings carried along while writing: e.g. the joy that I will have something beautiful for Max's Arcadia, thoughts about Freud of course, at one place about Arnold Beer, at another about Wassermann, one (to crush) Werfel's giantess, of course also about my "The Urban World".
>
> from Franz Kafka's diaries (23. 9. 1912)

... but he loved Thomas Mann's *Tonio Kröger* and eagerly sought out each line of this author in the *Neue Rundschau*, he read Hamsun, Hesse, Flaubert, Kassner with enthusiasm; his favourite writers later in life I can name: Emil Strauss, Wilhelm Schäfer, Carossa, further Hebel's *Jewellery Box*, Fontane, Stifter, Wilhelm Speyer's *The Melancholy of the Seasons*, Gogol, Dostojevsky (among the works of Dostojevsky he regarded especially highly the novel *The Youth*, at that time published in German by the publisher Langen; at one time he enthusiastically read me a passage about begging and getting rich), Tolstoy, the novels of Strindberg – but above all Kleist (he read, especially splendidly, laughing and weeping, the *Anecdotes from the Last Prussian War*) and then again and again Goethe and the Bible.

Max Brod, *About Franz Kafka*

Besides that first outburst of productivity, this year, 1912, was also of special significance for Kafka, because while visiting Max Brod he met the 24–year-old shop-assistant Felice Bauer of Berlin.

THE HOME OF MAX BROD'S PARENTS
Skořepka 1, Praha 1

The bachelor Max Brod was at the time a postal clerk and lived in Skořepka until 1913, the year of his marriage. Franz Kafka often visited him there and would read his own texts to his friends. On a midsummer day in 1912, Kafka visited Brod in order to put the finishing touches to the texts of *Meditation* with him. On this day, Felice Bauer was also present.

> When I got to Brod's on July 13 she was sitting at the table and seemed to me to be a servant girl. And I was not at all curious as to who she was, but took her for

Franz Kafka with his first fiancée, Felice Bauer

granted at once. Bony, empty face that wore its emptiness openly. Bare neck. Blouse thrown on. Looked quite domestic, although she herself was not, as it turned out later, like that at all. ... An almost broken nose. Blonde, somewhat stiff, dull hair, strong chin. As I sat down I looked at her more closely for the first time; once I was sitting, I already had an unshakeable opinion.

from Franz Kafka's diaries (20. 8. 1912)

Soon a relationship developed which involved ups and – even more so – downs. Franz Kafka found himself in a delicate situation: on the one hand he saw in marriage, and the starting of a family, the basis for a middle-class life worth striving for; on the other hand, solitude was for him a seemingly indispensable condition for creative work. Kafka tried to accommodate both of these conflicting elements: the path to it was a kind of 'living together' in the form of letters. Hardly a day passed in which he did not send at least one letter to Felice. However, in spite of two engagements, it never came to marriage.

The flat of Max Brod's parents in Skořepka

Madam!

I just went to the Statthalterei, walked slowly there and back, it is a good distance, you cross the river to the other bank of the Vltava. I had resigned myself to not receiving a letter from you today because I had thought until now that if it does not come early, it cannot come any more. The last two days, for various reasons, I've been a bit sad and distracted and I stopped on my way back in the Belvederegasse – on one side of the street are blocks of flats, on the other the unusually high walls of the Waldstein Gardens – took, without giving it much thought, your letters out of my pocket, placed Max's letter, which really didn't matter much to me and which lay on top, on the bottom and read a few lines from your first letter.

Franz Kafka to Felice Bauer (1912)

I often complain that so few places in Prague, at least as far as I know, have links to you. The apartment near the Brods, the Schalengasse, the coal market, the Perlengasse, the Obstgasse, the Graben. Then also the café in Obecní dům, the breakfast room in the "Blue Star" and the Vestibule. That is little, my love, but this little, how it stands out for me on the map of the city.

Franz Kafka to Felice Bauer (1913)

I should alienate you, my sweetheart? I, who am dying at my table out of longing for you. I was washing my hands today outside in the dark landing when somehow the thought of you came over me so strongly that I had to step over to the window to find comfort at least in the grey sky. This is how I live. Franz

Franz Kafka to Felice Bauer (1913)

The following list clearly and impressively shows how very much Kafka wrestled with his fate as a husband-to-be:

List of all the things that speak for and against my marrying:

1. Inability to endure life alone, not an inability to live, on the contrary, it is even improbable that I would know how to live with someone, but I am incapable of enduring the rush of my own life, the demands on my person, the attack on my time and age, the vague surge of a desire to write, the sleeplessness, the proximity to insanity – I am incapable of enduring all of this alone. Of course, perhaps I add to this myself. My contact with F. will give my existence a greater power of resistance.

2. Everything makes me stop and think. Every joke in the jokebook, the memories of Flaubert and Grillparzer, the sight of the night-shirts on my parents' beds prepared for the night, Max's marriage. Yesterday my sister said: "Everyone who is married (of our acquaintances) is happy, I don't understand it." Even this remark made me think; I became afraid again.

3. I have to be alone a lot. Whatever I have accomplished is only a result of being alone.

4. I hate anything that does not refer to literature, discussions bore me (even when they do refer to literature), paying visits bores me, the joys and sufferings of my relatives bore me to the depths of my soul. Discussions trivialize everything I think to be important, serious, true.

5. Fear of union, of flowing over. Then I will never be alone again.

6. I was often a completely different person in front of my sisters – this was especially the case earlier – than in front of other people. Fearless, exposed, powerful, surprising, moved as otherwise only through writing. If only I could be so above all through my wife! But would this not then deprive me of writing? Of all things not that, not that!

7. Alone, I could perhaps really give up my job one day. Married, this would never be possible.

from Franz Kafka's diaries (21. 7. 1913)

139

Garden restaurant on Žofín (1870)

THE OPPELT HOUSE ON OLD TOWN SQUARE
Staroměstské náměstí 6 (today 5), Praha 1

As of November 1913, the Kafka family lived in a six-room flat in the so-called Oppelt House on the corner of Pařížska třída and the Old Town Square. Kafka could see into Pařížska třída from his room.

> Straight ahead in front of my window I have the great dome of the Russian church [St. Niklas] with its two towers, and between the dome and the next block of flats the view onto a small triangular piece of Laurenziberg with a very small church. On the left I can see the Town Hall with its tower sharply rising in its great mass and re-clining in a perspective that perhaps nobody has ever seen before.
>
> Franz Kafka to Grete Bloch (1913)

140

Parts of the Oppelt House were damaged during the Prague uprising in 1945. The building was rebuilt one storey smaller than the original. It therefore looks somewhat different today than it did during Kafka's time. But the flat of the Kafkas has remained virtually unchanged and today houses an office.

The Oppelt House on Old Town Square (before it was damaged in the war)

1914 – 1918
THE WAR YEARS

In May 1914, Kafka celebrated his engagement to Felice Bauer. Although he was fit for military service, his indispensability at the insurance company released Kafka from military obligation. After the outbreak of war, he had to mind his brother-in-law's factory, as the latter was drafted.

> Patriotic parade. The major's speech. Then disappearance, then reappearance and the German cry: "Long live our beloved Monarch!" I am standing there wearing a nasty expression. These parades are one of the most disgusting side-effects of the war. Coming from the Jewish merchants who are at once German, at once Czech, and actually admit it, but have never allowed themselves to shout it out as loudly as they do now. Naturally, they drag along some others. Well-organized it was. It is supposed to be repeated every evening, tomorrow Sunday, twice.
>
> from Franz Kafka's diaries (6. 8. 1914)

A tank column during World War I

On the theatres of World War I

The outbreak and course of World War I came to influence – or, better said, interfere with – Kafka's life in many respects. The temporary wish to become a soldier must be seen and understood in relation to his wish to alter his specific life-situation. Kafka was spared the Kaiser's military uniform for professional and, later, health reasons.

> I have no time. There is general mobilisation. K. and P. have been called up. Now I will receive the reward for my being alone. It is, however, hardly a reward, being alone brings only punishment. Still, I am little moved by all this misery and more resolute than ever. I will have to be at the factory in the afternoon, but I will not live at home because E. is moving in with us with the 2 children. But I will write despite everything, absolutely, it is my struggle for self-preservation.
>
> from Franz Kafka's diaries (31. 7. 1914)

> Germany has declared war on Russia. – Swimming-school in the afternoon.
>
> from Franz Kafka's diaries (2. 8. 1914)

Trench (1916)

Franz Kafka at 31 years of age

THE FLAT IN BÍLEK STREET
Bílková 10, Praha 1

Kafka was 31 years old when, in the summer of 1914, he moved temporarily into the flat of his sister Valli, who was away on holiday. From February 10 to the end of March 1915 he lived as the main tenant in a different flat of the same house. In Bílková Kafka began writing his novel *The Trial.*

> Kafka begins *The Trial*, the novel of the "dead city", as World War I breaks out. At this time, he lives in a small bachelor's flat in Bílkova, frome where he goes on his late-evening walks through the city. The picture has grown dark, Prague has lost its contours and concrete names. The time on the tower clock has advanced far; not only the city, but the entire world cloaks itself in darkness. In the novel, we glimpse the river, the bridge, the island in the river, but we do not experience more. Despite that, however, we feel that it is Prague, that the inscrutable atmosphere corresponds to the character of the city and its inner labyrinth.
>
> Josef Kroutvor, *Kafkas Stadt?*
> *Prag im Zyklus der toten Städte*

The novel's so-called cathedral scene contains a number of details that leads one to believe that Kafka had Prague's St. Vitus Cathedral in mind when he wrote, for example, about the statue of a saint whose silver gleam recalls the impressive St. Nepomuk memorial beneath a baldachin. Today this statue is still one of the most important sights in Prague and, like the statues on the Charles Bridge, can scarcely be imagined as not being a vital part of the iconography of a non-Catholic at the turn of the century. However, the Milan cathedral, which Kafka had visited earlier and described in his diary as the pure representation of architecture, must also have contributed to his conception.

Inside St. Vitus Cathedral (main nave)

In the distance a large triangle of candlelights twinkles on the main altar, K. would not have been able to say with certainty if he had already seen them earlier. Perhaps they had just then been lit. Sextons are professional sneaks, one does not notice them. When K. happened to turn around, he saw, burning not far behind him, a candle firmly fastened high up a column. As beautiful as this was for the illumination of the altar-pieces, which hung mostly in the darkness of the side altars, it was wholly insufficient, it increased, instead, the darkness.

Franz Kafka, The Trial

The end of *The Trial* is also linked to a Prague site. In the vicinity of today's Strahov Stadium there was once a quarry, and there Kafka enacted Josef K.'s execution.

So they quickly left the city, which in this direction adjoined the fields almost without transition. A small quarry, abandoned and barren, was located near a still wholly city house. The men halted here, either because this place had been their destination from the start or because they were too tired to walk any farther. They now released K., who waited silently, removed their top hats and, while looking around the quarry, wiped the sweat from their foreheads with handkerchiefs. Moonlight lay everywhere with its artlessness and tranquillity, which no other light possesses.

Franz Kafka, The Trial

I have nothing to lose and everything to gain if I resign my job and leave Prague. I risk nothing, for my life in Prague leads to nothing good. ... Outside of Prague I can gain everything, that means I can become an independent, calm person who exploits all his abilities and for good and genuine work is rewarded with the feeling of being truly alive and enduringly satisfied.

Franz Kafka to his parents (1914)

In a letter to his fiancée Felice, Kafka recounted the story of his flat in Bílková:

An immense topic. It frightens me, I will not be able to cope with it. Too big for me. I will only be able to present a thousandth of it, and of that only a thousandth part will just be current for me as I write, and of that only a thousandth part will I be able to make comprehensible to you, and so on. Even so, it must be, I want to hear your advice. So read attentively and advise well: You know about my two-year suffering, small in relation to the simultaneous suffering of the world, but sufficient for me. A comfortable, friendly corner room, two windows, French windows. View of many roofs and churches. Tolerable people, since with a bit of practice I do not have to see them at all. Noisy street, heavy vehicles at the earliest hour, to which I have already almost become accustomed. The room is nevertheless uninhabitable for me. Of course, it lies at the end of a very long anteroom and is at first glance isolated enough, but it is a concrete building, I can hear – or, rather, heard – the sighing of the neighbours well past 10 o'clock, the conversations of those living below, now and then a banging from the kitchen. Besides, above the thin ceiling of the room is the attic, and it is unpredictable on which late afternoons, just when I would want to do some work, a servant girl hanging laundry innocently steps on my skull with the heel of her boot. Now and then there is also piano playing and in the summer, from the semi-circle of the other closely built houses, singing, a violin and a gramophone. So complete silence only from 11 o'clock at night. So the impossibility of coming to rest, complete homelessness, breeding ground for all illusions, ever greater weakness and hopelessness. How much more there is to say about it!

Franz Kafka to Felice Bauer (1915)

In "Blumfeld, an Elderly Bachelor", written in this apartment, Kafka, then a 32–year-old bachelor, referred not only to the noise in the flat, against which he felt completely helpless, but also suggested what his solitary evenings in the apartment were like:

> One evening, Blumfeld, an elderly bachelor, ascended to his flat, a strenuous undertaking because he lived on the sixth floor. During his climb, he thought – as he had often done recently – how burdensome this wholly solitary life was, that to reach his empty room he must climb these six storeys in absolute secrecy, there again in absolute secrecy don his nightgown, light the pipe, read a French newspaper to which he had subscribed for years, sip the cherry brandy he had poured for himself and, finally, after a half-hour, go to bed after rearranging the bedclothes, which the cleaning-woman, who was immune to every instruction, threw down according to her whim.
>
> Franz Kafka, *Description of a struggle and other writings not published in his Lifetime*

HOUSE "AT THE GOLDEN PIKE"
Dlouhá 18 (today 16), Praha 1

In February 1915, the same year *The Metamorphosis* was published, Franz Kafka moved into a flat in which he would remain until February 28, 1917. Kafka comments on this flat in Dlouhá to his former fiancée, Felice Bauer:

> I have moved into a room in which the noise is about ten times worse than in the previous one, but which is, in all other respects, incomparably more beautiful. I thought I was independent of the location and appearance of the room. But I'm not. Without a clearer view, without the possibility of seeing a greater piece of sky from my window and even a tower in the distance, even if it cannot be

Kafka residence „At the Golden Pike"

some open country, without this I am a miserable, dejected person; of course, I cannot say just what amount of misery is to be ascribed to the room, but it cannot be little; I even get the morning sun in this room, and as there are much lower roofs all around, it comes fully and straight in to me. But I have not only the morning sun, for it is a corner room and two windows face south-west. But, so that I do not get in too high spirits, there is someone in heavy boots who stomps back and forth above me until evening in an empty studio, and has set up some sort of useless noise machine there besides, which gives rise to the illusion of a bowling alley. Swiftly propelled, a heavy ball rolls the entire length of the ceiling, strikes the corner and rolls back, crashing heavily.

> Franz Kafka to Felice Bauer (1915)

Actually, it was neither heavy boots nor a useless machine, but rather

> ... the resonance of the whole damned concrete building ... On the floor above the room the machinery of the elevator whirrs and resounds through the empty attic space. (That is the previously imagined studio ghost, but there are also servant girls there who literally scrape the top of my skull with their slippers while drying the laundry).

> Franz Kafka to Felice Bauer (1915)

THE HOUSE IN THE GOLDEN LANE
Zlatá ulička 22, Praha 1

In the summer of 1916, after having spent a vacation in Marienbad (Mariánské lázně) with Felice Bauer, Kafka began to look around for a quiet place to write. He set out on a flat hunt with his favourite sister, Ottla, to the Golden Lane at Prague Castle, among other places.

I once went looking for a flat with Ottla in the summer, I no longer believed in the possibility of real quiet, nevertheless I went looking. We had a look at something in the Kleinseite, me the whole time thinking whether there were, in one of the old chateaux in an attic corner somewhere, a quiet hole where I could finally stretch out in peace. Nothing, we found nothing concrete. Just for fun we asked in the little lane. Yes, there would be a little house to let in November. Ottla, who also seeks quiet, though in her way, fell in love with the idea of renting the house ...

It had many flaws from the beginning, I do not have enough time to describe its development. Today it suits me completely. All in all: the lovely path up, the quiet there, only a very thin wall separates me from my neighbour, but the neighbour is quiet enough; I carry my supper up there and am usually there until midnight; then the departure and the walk home: I have to decide to stop, I then take the path that cools my head. And life there: it is something special to have one's own house, to lock the door to the world not of the room, not of the flat, but right of the house itself; to step out of the door of one's home straight into the snow of the quiet lane. All of it twenty crowns per month, supplied with all the

The Golden Lane at the Prague Castle

necessities by my sister, delivered by the little flower girl (Ottla's pupil) as inconspicuously as necessary, everything in order and beautiful.

Franz Kafka to Felice Bauer (1917)

... following it you reach an interesting piece of Old Prague, the so-called Alchemist Lane [The Golden Lane] with a dead-end at both ends of the street. Little houses are built along the wall stretching the distance of the Hirschgraben (formerly the connecting passage between the black and the white towers) where the alchemists lived at the time of Rudolf II.

Griebens Reiseführer Prag, 1911

The house has an unusually beautiful cellar with a window that gives out on Hirschgraben (Jelení příkop). Like the impressive attic, the cellar can be reached via a steep stairway. In the room on the ground floor of No. 22, which you enter through a tiny anteroom, there is now a small bookstore.

Inside Kafka's little house

Descent to the cellar   In the cellar of No. 22

The attic of No. 22

Beginning in late autumn of 1916, Kafka wrote a series of important texts at this romantic place, including the stories that would be published in 1920 in the collection *A Country Doctor*. After he had completed his day's work, Kafka usually spent evenings in the small house in the Golden Lane. He could not spend his nights in that small room, so he would leave in the early morning hours or go near "midnight down the old Castle Stairs into the city" and return across the then newly-built Mánes Bridge and Karpfengasse [Kaprova] to his Old Town flat.

> After your departure, there was a great storm in the Hirschgraben, perhaps by coincidence, perhaps on purpose. Yesterday I overslept in the Palais; when I came up into the house the fire was already out and it was very cold. Aha, I thought, the first evening without her and already lost. But then I took all the newspapers and manuscripts and, after a while, a very lovely fire was burning.
>
> Franz Kafka to his sister Ottla (1917)

THE SCHÖNBORN PALACE
Tržiště 15, Praha 1

In March 1917 Kafka rented, in addition to the workroom in the Golden Lane, a flat in the Schönborn Palace on the second floor.

> The count's Schönborn Palace, Tržiště 15 (beautiful frescoes), with a garden, which descends right down to the lower part of Petřín and which offers a wonderful view from its high-lying gloriette. Announce your entrance to the porter. Kleinseitner Ring [Malostranské náměstí] is not far from here.
>
> *Griebens Reiseführer Prag*, 1911

The Schönborn Palace (today, the American Embassy)

At about that time I returned from Munich with new courage, went into a housing agency, where almost the first thing I was told of was a flat in one of the most beautiful chateaux. Two rooms, an anteroom half of which was fitted out as the bathroom. Six hundred crowns annually. It was like a dream come true. I went there. High and beautiful rooms, red and gold, almost like in Versailles. Four windows in a courtyard submerged in absolute quiet, a window on the garden. The garden! When you enter the gateway of the palace you can hardly believe your eyes. Through the high semi-circle of the second gate flanked by caryatids you can see, when standing on the beautifully divided, curving stone steps of the large garden, a wide slope slowly and broadly climbing right up to a gloriette. Now, the flat had a small flaw. The previous tenant, a young man separated from his wife, had with his servant kept house for only a few months in the flat, was then unexpectedly transferred (he is a civil servant), and had to leave Prague, but in that short time he had already invested so much in the flat that he did not want to give it up just like that. That is why he kept it and was looking for someone who would replace his outlay (installation of electric lights, fitting out of the bathroom, the built-in cupboards, installation of the telephones, a large wall-to-wall carpet) at least in part. I was not this somebody.

For this he was asking (certainly little enough) six hundred and fifty crowns. It was too much for me, the excessively high ceilings of the rooms were also too magnificent for me, after all I did not even have any furniture, and there were smaller considerations, too. But now in the same palace there was another flat to let from the agency, on the second floor, with lower ceilings, a view onto the street, and the Hradschin right up to the windows. Friendlier, more human, modestly furnished; a countess, probably with more modest requirements, had stayed here as a guest, the girlish arrangement of old furniture was still standing there. But there were doubts

The Schönborn Palace, view into the garden

as to whether the flat was available. At the time that made me desperate. And just now it has been decided that the flat in the palace is available to me after all. The agent, whom I did a favour, is very friendly to me. I am getting the flat with the view onto the street for six hundred, albeit unfurnished, as I had anticipated. There are two rooms and an anteroom. There is electric light, though no bathroom, no bathtub, but I do not really need it. And now a little about the advantages of the present situation in comparison to the palace flat: 1. the advantage of everything-stays-as-it-was, 2. I am now content, why possibly cause myself regrets, 3. loss of my own house, 4. losing my way in the night, which improves my sleep, 5. I would have to borrow furniture from my sister now living with us; for the room, which is gigantic, I would actually have only one bed. The cost of moving, 6. I now live about ten minutes closer to the office. The palace flat faces to the west, I think, and my room has the morning light.

On the other hand, the advantages of the palace flat: 1. the advantage of change in general and change in particular, 2. the advantage of having one's own quiet flat, 3. I am not very independent in my current work flat anyway, actually I am depriving Ottla of it. As sacrificing and kind as she is to me, when she is in a worse mood she would, in time, still let it be known against her will. Mind you, she would certainly be sorry if I did not come to the little house anymore, basically it suffices her now and then to be there in the afternoon and on Sundays until 6 o'clock, 4. It is true that I will not have the way back home and going out at night will be difficult, since the gate cannot be unlocked from the outside, but in that section of the park otherwise reserved for the nobility, I can take a walk for a little while instead, 5. after the war I will still try, at first, to get a year-long holiday, that will soon not be possible, if at all. Thus we two would have prepared the most wonderful flat in Prague for you that I can imagine, albeit only for a relatively short time during which you would have to do without your own kitchen and bathroom. Even so this would be my intention, and you could have a long rest for three months. And the indescribable park in the spring, summer (the nobility are away) or autumn. But I will not secure the flat right away, in case I move there, or (incredibly, all beyond the means of a civil servant) only pay one hundred and fifty crowns quarterly, and hardly get it anymore; actually I have already taken it, but the agent will certainly be happy to release me from the agreement, especially since, understandably, the matter does not in the slightest have the same significance for him as it has for me. How little I have said. So now judge, and soon.

Franz Kafka to Felice Bauer (1917)

On the night of August 12–13 Kafka suffered a haemorrhage in the Schönborn Palace. The suspicion of tuberculosis would soon become a diagnosed certainty. Kafka later wrote to his friend Milena:

It started about three years ago with a haemorrhage in the middle of the night. I got up, alert as one is with anything new (instead of remaining lying down, which, I later learned, were doctor's orders), a bit startled too, of course, went to the window and leaned out, went to the washstand, walked around the room, sat down on the bed – the whole time blood. But I was not at all unhappy about this, for I gradually got to know for one unclear reason that I would, provided that the bleeding stopped, sleep again for the first time after three or four years of almost sleepless nights. It stopped (and since then has never returned) and I slept the rest of the night. In the morning the servant girl came, of course (at that time I had a flat in Schönborn Palace), a good, almost self-sacrificing but extremely matter-of-fact girl, saw the blood and said: *"Pane doktore, s Vámi to dlouho nepotrvá"* (Doctor, you won't last too long.). But I was feeling better than ever, I went first to the office, and only in the afternoon to the doctor. The continuation of the story is immaterial.

Franz Kafka to Milena Jesenská (1920)

Nerudova Street in Malá Strana

It happened that his brain could no longer endure the worries and suffering inflicted upon it. It said: 'I give it up; but if there is anyone else here on whom something of the preservation of the whole depends, then perhaps he would not mind relieving me of some of my burden and things will be all right for a little while longer.' At that the lung volunteered.

Franz Kafka to Milena Jesenská (1920)

The first doctor he consulted diagnosed bronchitis. At the advice of Max Brod, Kafka let himself be examined by a specialist. Dr. Friedel Pick finally confirmed the X-ray findings: pulmonary apicitis. (Kafka's reaction: "That is a word just like saying piglet when you mean swine.")

Yesterday came a letter from Dr. Mühlstein (I had first notified him by letter that I had gone to Professor P., also enclosed a copy of the diagnosis) in which, among other things, he writes: You can certainly expect to recover (!) but it will be noticeable only over long periods of time.

In this way my prospects have gradually dimmed through him. After the first examination I was almost healthy, after the second it was even better, later a mild bronchitis on the left side, still later, "not to minimize or maximize anything", tuberculosis right and left, which however would quickly be cured in Prague, and now, finally, I can one day certainly expect to recover. It is as if he wanted to hide from me with his broad back the Angel of Death, who is standing behind him, and as if he is now gradually stepping aside. Neither of them (unfortunately?) frightens me.

Franz Kafka to Felix Weltsch (1917)

Tuberculosis – that was the diagnosis with which Franz Kafka could hope to obtain early retirement in order to devote himself entirely to his writing. Although his September 6, 1917, application for retirement was rejected, he was granted a three-month convalescence leave, which he spent at his sister Ottla's in the North Bohemian town of Zürau (Siřem).

Following this, he gave up his two residences in Prague. During his (increasingly infrequent) stays in Prague, Kafka now lived with his parents in the Oppelt House .

In July of this memorable 1917 Kafka got engaged for a second time to Felice Bauer. The final break-up, which followed on the heels of this engagement, came during the Christmas

The Old Castle Stairway (around 1895)

holidays of the same year. When the asbestos factory was liquidated, Kafka could divest himself of his share in the enterprise, and therefore of another fragment of the bourgeois lifestyle.

Since the convalescence leave was prolonged until April 1918, Kafka was able to return to Ottla in Šírem.

Kafka's sister Ottla with her husband

The Týn courtyard and Ungelt, with the Týn Church in the background

Although Prague at most appears in occasional paraphrases in Kafka's work, it nevertheless exists everywhere in his writing, like the salt in the water of the Buddhist parables.

Johannes Urzidil, *There Goes Kafka*

1919
After World War I

In October 1918, Kafka fell seriously ill with the Spanish flu. Although he retrurned to work in November, additional convalescence periods were necessary. He travelled to Pension Stüdl in Schelesen, near Liboch on the Elbe, and also spent the first months of 1919 there.

There he met the 30-year-old Julie Wohryzek, with whom he spent a lot of time in the spring and summer. Although they soon celebrated their engagement, this relationship, too, did not lead to marriage and dissolved in autumn because of Kafka's misgivings. Here, his now well-to-do father's disapproval of a bride with a modest background played only a secondary role.

> Was in Rieger Park [Riegrovy sady]. Walked up and down past the small jasmine bushes with J. False and

View of Prague from Rieger Park

real, false in sighing, real in togetherness, in trust, in feeling safety. Restless heart.

from Franz Kafka's diaries (30. 6. 1919)

Monday holiday at the Baumgarten [Stromovka], in the restaurant on the gallery. Suffering and joy, guilt and innocence like two inextricably clasped hands, one would have to cut through flesh, bone and blood.

from Franz Kafka's diaries (8. 12. 1919)

Thursday. Cold. Silent with J. in Rieger Park. Seduction in the Graben. All this is too difficult. I am not well-enough prepared. Intellectually it is as when, 26 years ago, the teacher Beck said, without however noticing the prophetic joke: "But let him go into the fifth class, he's too weak, this haste will revenge itself later". In fact, I

Former restaurant in Baumgarten (Stromovka), around 1885

grew up like seedlings that have been forced up too
quickly and forgotten, a certain artistic fragility in the
evasionary movements when a breeze come.

from Franz Kafka's diaries (11. 12. 1919)

In 1919, after a two-year pause in his creativity, Kafka wrote a
work that would mark the zenith of his artistic production.
Letter to his father, which the 36-year-old son wrote in
November of that year, during another stay in Schelesen – this
time Max Brod came along – was the attempt to come to
terms with his overbearing father.

> Dearest Father,
> You once asked me recently why I claim to be afraid of
> you. I did not know, as usual, what to answer, partly out
> of my fear of you and partly because the cause of this fear
> consists of too many details for me to put even halfway
> into words. And if I try to answer you in writing here, it
> will be only very incomplete anyway, because even in
> writing my fear and its consequences inhibit me toward
> you, and because the magnitude of the material far ex-
> ceeds my memory and my understanding.
>
> Franz Kafka, *Letter to his father*

Like the faded monarchy, newly created Czechoslovakia was a
multinational state in which the majority ethnic group had
the greatest say, but under altered conditions. Although the
waves of anti-Semitism of the early years of the First Republic
were nothing new, they were nevertheless remarkable and of
astonishing intensity, especially in view of the clear repudia-
tion of these tendencies by President T. G. Masaryk, who was
very popular. But even Masaryk, who as a lawyer had acted on
behalf of a Jew unjustly accused of committing a ritual murder
and in the process put his career on the line, could not prevent
the violence of the frenzied mobs.

> Every afternoon I now walk along the streets and bathe
> in anti-Semitism. "Prašivé plemeno" [filthy race] I have
> now once heard the Jews referred to. Is it not absolutely

Tomáš Garrigue Masaryk, the first Czechoslovak president

obvious that you leave behind the place where you are hated (Zionism or nationalist sentiment are not necessary for that at all)? The heroism that consists in staying anyway is that of the cockroaches which cannot even be exterminated from the bathroom.

I have just looked out of the window: mounted police, gendarmerie with their bayonets ready to attack, the screaming masses running in all directions, and up here at the window the revolting disgrace of having to live the whole time in refuge.

Franz Kafka to Milena Jesenská (1920)

It is as if before every walk someone must not only wash and comb himself, etc. – that is already strenuous enough – but also, because before every walk he always lacks all the necessities, sew his jacket, repair the shoes, make the hat, carve the walking-stick, etc. Of course, he cannot do any of this well, it all holds together for perhaps a few blocks, but in Na Příkopě, e.g., everything suddenly falls apart and he stands there naked with only scraps and fragments. Then the torture of returning to Old Town Square. And in the end he comes upon a mob that is hunting Jews. Don't misunderstand me, Milena, I am not saying that this man is lost, absolutely not, but he is lost when he walks in Na Příkopě, there he disgraces himself and the world.

Franz Kafka to Milena Jesenská (1920)

THE FORMER KORNHÄUSER CARPENTER'S WORKSHOP IN PRAGUE-KARLÍN
Šaldova 5 (formerly Poděbradgasse), Praha 8

To compensate for his office job and also as part of his vision of a natural life, Franz Kafka occupied himself with a variety of utilitarian activities alongside his job at the insurance company (e.g. as assistant gardener in the Dvorský nursery). He also tried his hand at carpentry in Karlín, among other things. Gustav Janouch tells about this in his memoirs *Gespräche mit Kafka* (Discussions with Kafka) :

> We got into conversation and he confessed to me that he was "taking classes" from the carpenter Kornhäuser in Poděbradgasse in Karolinenthal (Karlín) in the afternoons after office hours.... During my next visit with Kafka, I asked:
> "Are you still going to the carpenter's in Karolinenthal?"
> "You know about that?"
> "My father told me."
> "No, I havn't been going for quite a while. His Majesty the body."
> "I can imagine. Work in the dusty workshop is nothing pleasant."
> "You're wrong about that. I love the work in the workshop. The smell of planed wood, the singing of the saw, the blows of the hammer, it all captivates me. The afternoon would fade away just like that. The evening would amaze me."
> "You must have been tired."
> "I was tired, but also happy. There is nothing lovelier than such a craft. Besides the workshop I have also worked in agriculture. That was all much nicer and more valuable than the drudgery at the office. There you are apparently something higher, better, but it is merely appearance. In reality, you are only lonelier and thus more unhappy. That's all. Intellectual work tears people from human society. Craft, on the other hand, leads them to others. It's a shame that I can no longer work in the workshop or the garden."

The former Kornhäuser carpentry workshop in Karlín

1920 – 1922
YEARS OF ILLNESS

In 1920 Kafka"s relationship and correspondence with the Czech intellectual Milena Jesenská began. The 24-year-old Jesenská had already expressed an interest in 1919 in translating Kafka's "The Stoker" into Czech. This was a new experience for Kafka, as neither Felice Bauer nor Julie Wohryzek had worked up an understanding of or even interest in his writings. The passionate relationship with Jesenská, a medical student who lived in Vienna and was miserable in her unhappy marriage with the Prague bon vivant and café writer Ernst Polak, ultimately became just another confirmation for Kafka of his fundamental inability to establish a permanent relationship with a woman.

> Please write the address a little more clearly. Hardly is your letter in the envelope and it is almost my property and you should treat someone else's property with more care, more sense of responsibility. *Tak* [So]. By the way, I also have the impression, without being able to determine it more precisely, that a letter of mine has got lost. The anxiety of the Jews! Instead of fearing that the letters arrive safely!
>
> Franz Kafka to Milena Jesenská (1920)

On December 18, 1920, Kafka began a long rest and fattening cure in Matliary, Slovakia. There, in the tuberculosis sanatorium in the High Tatra mountains, he met Robert Klopstock, also ill with tuberculosis, who would remain a close friend until Kafka's death. When Klopstock later moved to Prague – and did not at all feel at home there – Kafka recommended that he move to Berlin since Prague's worth was "dubious".

Milena Jesenská (with her tennis trainer)

In February 1922 Kafka, for whom the publication of his works meant less all the time, began work on the novel *The Castle*, which would never be completed. By August the first nine chapters had been completed. From Jan. 27 until Feb. 17, Kafka recuperated in Spindlermühle (Špindlerův mlýn) in the Riesengebirge (Krkonoše), still a favourite destination for Prague winter-sports lovers today.

Kafka had long wanted to give up his detestable job at the insurance company, and his wish now was gradually fulfilled, first because of his long convalescence leaves, from which it was always difficult to return to Prague, and finally early retirement, which was definitively granted as of July 1, 1922.

Kafka's health scarcely improved as a result of the various cures and sanatorium stays. Just after his retirement, he spent the summer of 1922 with his favourite sister, Ottla, in Planá nad Lužnicí. Ottla gave her noise-sensitive brother a large room, while she stayed in a smaller room with her young daughter, Věra.

The Mánes gallery

It is Kafka's almost satiric credit that the Prague that ended with him was not buried with him. ...

Johannes Urzidil, *There Goes Kafka*

178

1923 – 1924
The Final Years in Berlin, Prague and Kierling near Vienna

Kafka's final years were characterised by his constantly deteriorating health and the related stays in sanatoria and rest cures.

By spring 1923 Kafka was mostly bed-ridden. In May he took a holiday in Dobřichovice, and spent the summer in the Baltic spa of Müritz, where he met his last love, the solicitous Dora Diamant. Already on September 24 of the same year, Kafka moved to Dora in Berlin. If only briefly, Kafka experienced with Dora the semblance of a happy amorous relationship and, at least for a while, escaped his demons. In Berlin Kafka also spent time with the physician and writer Ernst Weiss. When he was strong enough, Kafka visited the College for Jewish Science.

Kafka also felt the hardship of the 1923 summer of inflation. His health deteriorated. Alarmed by the news of Kafka's condition, which Dora Diamant conveyed to Franz's parents, Dr. Siegfried Löwy came to Berlin and talked the reluctant Kafka into returning to Prague. In March 1924, accompanied by Max Brod, Kafka came home and remained there for about three weeks. His health continued to deteriorate; the tuberculosis spread to his larynx. In April, Kafka travelled to Austria to be treated by a specialist.

After stays at the sanatorium Wiener Wald in Lower Austria and one week at the Vienna General Hospital (the laryngeal clinic of Dr. Hajek), Franz Kafka entered the sanatorium of Dr. Hoffmann in Kierling near Vienna, where he was nursed by his friend Robert Klopstock and Dora Diamant. He spent the last six weeks of his life in this sanatorium. During this time he lost the use of his voice and was confronted with the harrowing hopelessness of his condition.

Kafka, who in the end could only communicate by means of slips of paper and was suffering from constant pain and thirst, passed away on the morning of June 3, 1924.

The funeral took place eight days later, at 4 p.m. on June 11, at the New Jewish Cemetery in Prague-Strašnice. His coffin was accompanied by the writer's family, Dora Diamant, who was supported by Max Brod, and several acquaintances.

THE NEW JEWISH CEMETERY IN PRAGUE-STRAŠNICE
(Nový Židovský hřbitov)
Nad vodovodem 1, Praha 3

One of Prague's largest cemeteries, it was laid out in 1881. Such distinguished turn-of-the-century architects as Antonín Balšánek, Jan Kotěra and Josef Zasche designed gravestones for this cemetery. To the right of the

Hebraic inscription in the Old-New Synagogue

entrance, about 200 m from the porter's lodge, is the grave of Franz Kafka with inscriptions in German and in Hebrew.

Hugo Rokyta, *Die Böhmischen Länder: Prag*

I walked in the funeral procession that brought Kafka's coffin from the ceremonial hall to the open grave; I went with his friends behind his family and his pale companion, who was supported by Max Brod. They were all still quite young at the time, at least the oldest (Brod, Hugo Bergmann and Oskar Baum) were only in their early forties; Felix Weltsch, Ludwig Winder, Rudolf Fuchs and Friedrich Thieberger (my brother-in-law and Kafka's Hebrew teacher) were still in their thirties, I was in my twenty-ninth year. Only a few of the hundred or so people who marched with us under the willows and cypresses on that day are still alive and can testify to Kafka's paradigmatic world significance. As the coffin sank, Dora Diamant cried out excruciatingly and piercingly, but her sobs, which, of course, could only be appreciated by him for whom they were meant, veiled the dying sound of the Hebrew Prayer for the Dead, which announces the glory of God and the profound hope of redemption.

"Writing as a form of prayer", that was Kafka's definition of the writer; and: "Even if no redemption comes, I still want to be worthy of it every moment", this was his belief. We threw dirt into the grave. I can remember the dirt very clearly. It was light, coarse, loamy earth mixed with crumbling pieces of stone and pebbles that fell on the coffin with a loud rumbling. Then the mourners dispersed. I left with my wife, who had known Kafka as a neighbour since childhood, and with the translator Rudolf Fuchs. No one said a word. Finally, rain began to fall from the murky sky.

Johannes Urzidil, *There Goes Kafka*

Ceremonial hall at the New Jewish Cemetery

In the first obituary, published in the *Prager Tagblatt* June 24, 1924, Max Brod honoured his late friend:

> Where to begin? - It doesn't matter. Because one of the particularities of this figure is that you come to the same conclusion from every approach. - And from this it follows that honesty, unshakeable authenticity, is purity. Because the lie offers a different sight to each side, and the impure changes colour. But with Franz Kafka – and I would almost say only with him in the entire circle of the literary modern – there is no change of colour, no change of prospect, no shifting of the scenery. Here is truth and nothing but the truth.
>
> Max Brod

A number of other Prague and German, particularly Berlin, newspapers announced Kafka's death or published obituaries. Among them were the *Prager Abendblatt* (obituary by Rudolf Fuchs), the *Prager Presse* (obituary by Oskar Baum; a few days later followed a 'poet's tribute' by Otto Pick), the *Berliner Tagblatt*, the *Berliner Börsenkurier*, the *Vossische Zeitung* and the *Frankfurter Zeitung*. In the Jewish newspaper *Selbstwehr*, Kafka's schoolmate Felix Weltsch published a commemorative page for the deceased in which it was declared that he had been 'a Jew with strong bonds to Judaism, a burning Zionist'.

The following obituary was published by Anton Kuh in *Die Stunde* one week after Kafka's death and after the entire Austrian press, preoccupied with the assassination of Chancellor Ignaz Seipel, had ignored the writer's death.

> Let us suppose that the great national writer Hans Müller or his clever little brother Lothar – or: Anton Wildgans, Karl Schönherr, Karl Hans Strobl – let us suppose one of these oft-quoted one day closes his eyes never to wake again – supposing, I say-what a buzzing and humming there would be, since the froth is already spraying up high around the living.
>
> The "Mutual Insurance Company of Names" representing the dull, the dumb and the sedentary at the newspaper level just goes on functioning promptly and efficiently.

But a few days ago, a writer died; one of those whose life will seem ever more important in the future than in his time; one of those about whom, on the occasion of the tenth, fiftieth or hundredth anniversary of his death, the Müllers, Lothars e tutti quanti will write fine, flowery feature pages with a lasting message

He died and there was not a cock who crowed after him. Not one of them was so moved as to write even ten columns.

Why?

Out of a lack of literary education? Or because the deceased was to be included in the noble minority and not those who curry favour among the papers?

Perhaps. But the main reason most certainly is that this Franz Kafka, in whose outwardly scant work language finally wears a face again, nowhere gives substance to the affected adoration and currying of favours because he lives in his "Yes" as well as in his "No" so completely beyond the world of newspapers, an occupant of the lonely three-dimensional nature of art. Later they will compare his life (during his last ten years he lay almost uninterrupted in bed) to that of Pascal's; they will expose connections between his accounts of dreams-become-story and psychoanalysis; the name Kleist will crown the comparisons.

Today they do not even prove themselves worthy of the honour which he who originated in Prague did Vienna in that he spent his last days a few kilometres from our city and died there.

Kierling bei Klosterneuburg has entered literary history through him. (The town Weidlich too enjoys this honour through the grave of Lenau.)

But the feature writers, for whom such a connection otherwise gives an opportunity to cook a broth out of a cabby's song and Mount Olympus, Parnassus and the Viennese forest, have missed this deadline.

For Franz Kafka had no petty allegiances.

Anton Kuh

His funeral. The prayer-hall of the Jewish cemetery in Prague. Great participation. Hebrew prayers. The grief of his parents and sisters. The silent despair of his companion, who falls down as though dead at his grave. The gloomy weather, which only brightens in brief moments. God knows one could not believe that in the bare, wooden chest, Franz Kafka is being buried, the writer who has only recently started to become great.

Rudolf Fuchs

The day before yesterday Dr. Franz Kafka, a German writer who lived in Prague, died in the sanatorium of Kierling near Klosterneuburg near Vienna. Only a few people here knew of him, for he was a loner, a person aware of and frightened by the world; he had been suffering from tuberculosis for many years, and even if he had cured it, he still consciously nourished it and encouraged it in his thoughts. . . . It lent him an almost unbelievable sensitivity and an almost terribly uncompromising intellectual refinement. . . . He wrote the most important books in recent German literature; the wrestling of today's generation of the entire world is in them, even if they are without tendentious words. They are true, naked and painful, so that even where they express themselves symbolically, they are virtually naturalistic. They are full of the dry scorn and sensitive observations of a person who has perceived the world so clearly that he could not endure it and was forced to die.

Milena Jesenská

The beautiful Cubist tombstone that adorns Franz Kafka's final resting-place, as well as that of his parents, Hermann and Julie, was designed by the Prague architect Leopold Ehrmann. On the wall opposite the grave (Site No. 21 14 21), a simple commemorative plaque recalls Kafka's lifelong friend and mentor, Max Brod. In 1937, many years after Kafka's death, Ernst Weiss wrote to Max Brod:

I never stopped trying to estrange him from Prague. You – as a true and wonderful friend, for which I envy K. – kept him there. The diaries showed me that he was trapped there in a tragic manner. You therefore had to win, and he had to die there.

Even after his death, Kafka could not free himself of Prague, although he had gone to Vienna to die.

The writer's grave in the New Jewish Cemetery – long a shrine for literary pilgrims – remains not only one of the most important Kafka memorials in Prague, but also one of the most tranquil and impressive.

Commemorative plaque for Max Brod

The Kafka family's Cubist tombstone

THE FIST IN THE COAT OF ARMS

In the beginning everything was in passable order for the building of the tower of Babel; indeed the organisation was perhaps overdone, too much thought was given to the guides, interpreters, workers' accommodations and connecting roads as if centuries of undisturbed working opportunities lay ahead. The prevailing opinion of that time even went so far as to say that one could not build slowly enough; this opinion did not need to be overemphasised in the least, and people could shrink away from laying the foundations at all. The argument went as follows: the essence of this whole undertaking is the idea of building a tower which will reach heaven. Against this idea everything else is of secondary importance. Once grasped in its entirety, the idea cannot vanish again; as long as there are people, there will also be the strong desire to finish the building of the tower. But in this regard there is no need to worry about the future; on the contrary, human knowledge is increasing, architecture has made progress and will continue to make progress, a task for which we need a year will perhaps be accomplished in half a year a hundred years from now, and moreover be more durable. Why then toil away now to the limit of one's powers? That would only make sense if one could hope to raise the tower in the span of one generation. But this is in no way to be expected. More likely, the succeeding generation with its improved knowledge would find the work of the previous generation poor and tear down what had been built and begin anew. Such thoughts caused energies to flag and people concerned themselves more with the building of a city for workers than the building of the tower.

Each association wanted to have the best quarter; thus conflicts arose which escalated into bloody battles. These battles continued ceaselessly. To the leaders this provided a new argument for building the tower very slowly, due to the lack of necessary concentration, or preferably only after a peace agreement had been reached. However, time was not just spent fighting; in the intervals the city was improved, which admittedly provoked new envy and new conflicts. Thus the period of the first generation passed, but none of the following were any different. Skills increased steadily and with them the addiction to fighting ...

In addition, the second or third generation already understood the senselessness of the tower suicide mission, though they were already far too closely bound up with one another to leave the city. All the legends and songs which have originated in this city are filled with the longing for the prophesied day on which the city will be smashed to pieces by five successive blows from a gigantic fist. This is also why the city has the fist on its coat of arms.

Franz Kafka, *On the Problem of our Laws and Other Writings Unpublished in his Lifetime*

The Prague coat of arms

ACKNOWLEDGEMENT
FOR THE ILLUSTRATIONS

The publisher and the author wish to thank:

Prof. Hartmut Binder for his generosity in allowing us to publish illustrations from his archives and which appear on pages 48, 64, 100, 136, 146, 165, 176;

The Prague photographer Ivan Koreček for the photos on pages 86, 131, 178, 180, 187;

And Dr. Jindřich Noll for permission to use the historic map of the city of Prague.

The remaining illustrations have been taken from the publisher's own collection of historic illustrations and publications.

EXPLICATION OF PLACE-NAMES

Since in his writings Kafka employed the German names for streets and other sites, as was customary for German residents of Prague at the time, these have also been used primarily in this book. However, because Prague has become an almost purely Czech city, the following index of the place-names that appear most often in this book have been translated into their Czech equivalents. Where places were renamed, the current name is given after the historic one.

GERMAN	CZECH
Altneusynagoge	Staronová synagoga
Altstadt	Staré město
Altstädter Rathaus	Staroměstska radnice
Altstädter Ring	Staroměstské náměstí
Aposteluhr	Orloj
Baumgarten	Stromovka
Burg	Hrad
Čechbrücke	Čechův most
Civilschwimmschule	Občanská plovárna
Deutsches Haus	Německý dům [today: Slovanský dům]
Eisengasse	Železná
Elisabethbrücke	Eliščin most
Ferdinandstraße	Ferdinandská [today: Národní třída]
Fleischmarkt	Masný trh
Geistgasse	Dušní
Goldenes Gäßchen	Zlatá ulička
Graben	Na Příkopě
Hasenburg	Nebozízek
Heinrichsgasse	Jindřišská
Hirschgraben	Jelení příkop
Hradschin	Hradčany
Hungermauer	Hladová zeď'
Hybernergasse	Hybernská
Jungmannstraße	Jungmanova
Karlsbrücke	Karlův most

Karlsgasse	Karlova
Karlsplatz	Karlovo náměstí
Karpfengasse	Kaprova
k.k.	c.k.
Kleiner Ring	Malé náměstí
Kleinseite	Malá strana
Kleinseitner Ring	Malostranské náměstí
Kloster Strahov	Klášter Strahov
Kohlmarkt	Uhelný trh
Königliche Weinberge	Královské Vinohrady
Kreuzherrenplatz	Křížovnické náměstí
Lange Gasse	Dlouhá
Laurenziberg	Petřín
Maislgasse	Maislova
Mánesbrücke	Mánesův most
Marktgasse	Tržíště
Neues Deutsches Theater	Nové německé divadlo [today: Státní opera]
Neustadt	Nové město
Niklasstraße	Mikulášská
Obstmarkt	Ovocný trh
Obstgasse	Ovocná
Perl[en]gasse	Perlova
Pulverturm	Brašná brána
Repräsentationshaus	Obecní dům
Riegerpark	Riegroy sady
Rudolfinum	Dům umělců
Salvatorkirche	Kostel sv. Salvatora
Schalengasse	Skořepka
Schützeninsel	Střelecký ostrov
Sixthaus	Sixtův dům
Sommerberg	Letná
Sophieninsel	Žofín
St. Niklaskirche	Chrám sv. Mikuláše
St. Veitsdom	Chrám sv. Víta
Staatsoper	Státní opera
Stadtpark	Městské sady
Teinkirche	Týnský chrám
Veitsdom	Katedrála sv. Víta
Wenzelsplatz	Václávské náměstí
Welsche Gasse	Vlašská
Zeltnergasse	Celetná
Ziegenplatz	Kozí náměstí

Map labels (visible on map):
Piseckà brana · Ul Pisecké brany · XVIII · Mariánské hradby · Král Anny zahrad pavill (Belvedere) · Chotkovy sady · 25 · Cisařská zahrada · XIX · 24 · Daliborka · Chotkova silnice · Cesta pod Letnou · Občanská plovárna · eni příkop · 26 · Bílá vž · Jiřská ul · Jiřská ul · Starý schody zámecké · Ústav šlechti · Fürstenberská zahrada · Pod Bruskou · Dojenská plovárna · Valdštynská zah. · Železná lávka · Klášter Anglických panen · C.k. zemsk zems soud · Os · Lk · J · Plátnerská · 27 · Pk · III · 23 · Most Karlúv · 15 · Pod Bruskou · Starom. Ml · Novotného lávka · Anenská ulice · Ostrov · PM Vítězné · Zlatá ulice · Bethemská · Kř · 28 · dráha · Café Louvre · Café Ferdinum · Újezd · čísaře Františka · KL Ursulinek · Ostrov · 15 · Lodecké M · Slítkovská · Šítkovská · V.

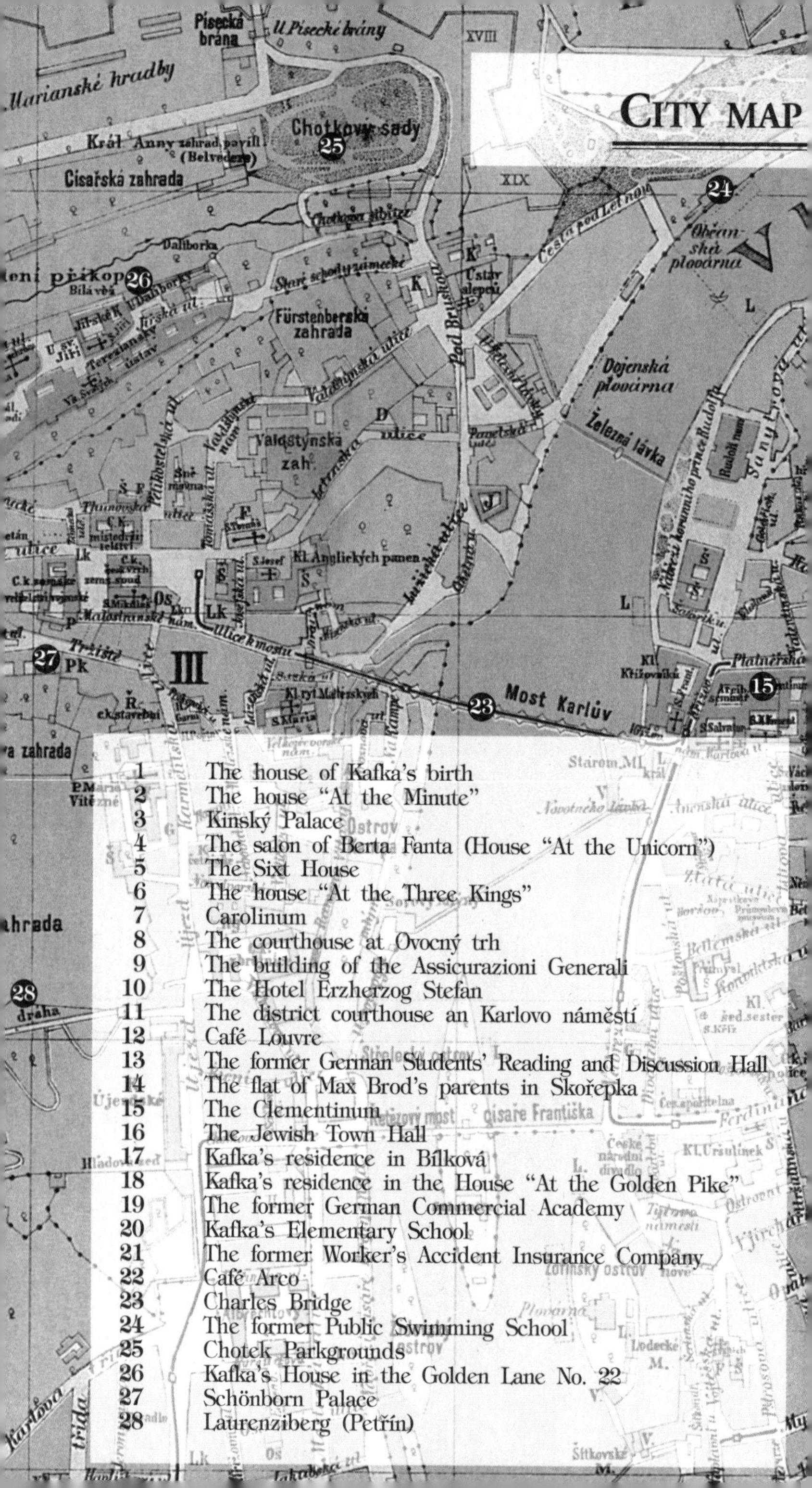

Legend: